To the Farewell Address

IDEAS OF EARLY AMERICAN
FOREIGN POLICY

TO
THE FAREWELL
ADDRESS

Ideas of Early American
Foreign Policy

BY

FELIX GILBERT

PRINCETON UNIVERSITY PRESS
PRINCETON, NEW JERSEY

Foreword

THE inception of this book goes back to a seminar on "American Isolationism" held at the Institute for Advanced Study in Princeton during 1939-1940. A first draft was near completion when the war interrupted further work.

Since I then became engaged in other tasks and it seemed doubtful whether I would be able to resume work on the manuscript, I published some results of my investigations in two articles: the one, entitled "The English Background of American Isolationism in the Eighteenth Century," appeared in *The William and Mary Quarterly* in 1944; the other, entitled "The 'New Diplomacy' of the Eighteenth Century," in *World Politics* in 1951. These articles form the substance of the second and third chapters of this book. I realized, however, that this piecemeal form of publication would not produce the full picture of the development, as I saw it, and I decided to wait and see whether an occasion for finishing the book, as it was originally planned, might not arise.

This opportunity came when I served as guest professor at the University of Cologne during the winter semester of 1959-1960 and lectured there on "The Beginnings of American Foreign Policy." I revised and completed the manuscript during my stay in Cologne. In research and writing I had the continuous collaboration of Mary Raymond Gilbert. I wish to thank Miss H. Riedel, the Librarian of the Amerika Institut at the University of Cologne, for help in procuring books, and Mrs. Fassnacht for typing the manuscript.

I am indebted to my colleagues in the History Departments of Bryn Mawr College, Haverford College, and the University of Pennsylvania—Arthur P. Dudden, Mary M. Dunn, Richard S. Dunn, Wallace T. MacCaffrey, and Caroline Robbins—for reading the entire manuscript and for giving helpful criticisms. I am grateful for the interest which

FOREWORD

Miss R. Miriam Brokaw, the Managing Editor of the Princeton University Press, has taken in my manuscript.

During the long, interrupted process of composition I have received valuable suggestions from a great number of friends and colleagues. If I do not list their names individually, this does not mean that I have not appreciated their assistance. Two of them, however, have played such an important role in the genesis of this book that it cannot be published without mention of them: Douglass Adair and the late Edward M. Earle. From the outset, Douglass Adair gave me advice in my researches and his constant questions about the progress of the manuscript did much to keep my interest in the work alive. Edward M. Earle organized the seminar which directed my attention to the problems of this book, and I shall always remain obligated to him for his enthusiastic encouragement and help.

FELIX GILBERT

Bryn Mawr College
February 1961

Contents

To the Farewell Address

IDEAS OF EARLY AMERICAN
FOREIGN POLICY

CHAPTER I

The Colonies and Europe

I

"WE ARE as near to Heaven by sea as by land." These are the last known words of Sir Humfrey Gilbert, the first Englishman who conceived of a settlement of English people on the North American continent. In the name of his Great Queen, Sir Humfrey had taken possession of New Foundland, which, he hoped, would provide riches for himself, his family, his friends, and his country. On his return voyage to England, a storm swept away part of his fleet, leaving only the *Golden Hind* and Sir Humfrey's flagship, the tiny *Squirrel*. Before these two ships were torn apart by another storm, in which the *Squirrel* foundered with all on board, the men of the *Golden Hind* could see Sir Humfrey sitting on the quarterdeck of the *Squirrel* and reading. What he read excited him to this exclamation.[1]

The book in Sir Humfrey's hands must have been the *Utopia* of Sir Thomas More, for it contains the thought which stimulated Sir Humfrey: "the way to heaven out of all places is of like length and distance." More's *Utopia* was a strangely fitting book for Sir Humfrey to read. Behind Sir Humfrey's plans for a settlement in New Foundland, there was not only the anticipation of gaining great wealth, but also the hope of

[1] Richard Hakluyt, *The Principal Voyages of the English Nation*, Everyman's Library, London 1926, vol. VI, p. 35.

creating an ideal life and society. Thus, the first Englishman who envisaged plantations of his countrymen on the North American continent was driven by two incentives which in the following centuries inspired the astounding growth of the English colonies. The promise of financial rewards and the belief in the possibility and necessity of constructing a more perfect social order were the two motives which led people to embark on the dangerous voyage to the New World. Different—almost contradictory—as these two motives were, they existed together, tightly intertwined in the development of the various English settlements on American soil.

Each motive implied one of two distinct and contrary attitudes to the Old World. The economic motive necessitated close ties with Europe. Great profits could result only from the cultivation and production of goods for export. Pursuit of these activities required bonds with England; business contacts with the London merchants and personal connections with members of the ruling aristocracy, who promoted colonial schemes in the expectation of quick enrichment, had to be maintained. The utopian motive favored separation from European affairs. The hope of leading a more perfect life on the new continent formed a resistance to involvements with Europe. The attempt to realize a better social order presupposed a critical view of the values of the Old World and aroused a fear of ties which might spread the diseases of Europe to America.

In New England, where the settlers had entered into a covenant with God, so that this area might be preserved as the only center of true religion, the Puritan leaders felt themselves worlds removed from other colonies. They looked down with contempt upon the manners and customs which the riches from tobacco production were creating in Virginia. Nothing worse could be imagined than that New England might become "like the rest of the Nations, being grown into the same conformity to the World, with other Plantations."[2]

It would be wrong, however, to accept the Puritans' own evaluation of New England's unique position. It should not be assumed that the religious plantations—Plymouth Colony, Massachusetts Bay, Rhode Island, and Connecticut—were fundamentally different from the rest of the English colonies on the North American continent. The power of the theocracy to subordinate worldly activities to the ideal of a society organized for the purposes of God weakened in New England even before the first generation of settlers had died. From the middle of the seventeenth century, the inhabitants of New England were frequently reminded by their ministers that "New England is originally a plantation of religion, not a plantation of trade."[3] Admonishments against vanity and the sinfulness of luxury, and warnings against the danger of forgetting the true aims of life, increased in number and vehemence in the course of the seventeenth century. At last, it came to be admitted that wealth and prosperity might be a sign of God's special regard for the people of New England who lived under the covenant. It had not been possible to restrict economic activities to farming; trade with other colonies and with England had become more and more important. A merchant class, occupied with worldly concerns and far-flung interests, began to play the leading role in the social life of New England.

Although originally the prevalence of a self-sufficing village economy in the North and of large plantations producing tobacco for export in the South had given the social life of North and South a different pattern, this dividing line soon became blurred. Nor was there a separation between

[2] Increase Mather, as quoted by Perry Miller, *The New England Mind: the Seventeenth Century*, New York 1939, p. 472.

[3] John Higginson, *The Cause of God and His People in New England*, as quoted by Thomas J. Wertenbaker, *The Puritan Oligarchy; the Foundation of American Civilization*, New York 1947, p. 202.

North and South because the settlement in these two regions had been undertaken for different motives. Not all the northern colonies were religious foundations, nor were all the southern colonies solely commercial enterprises. Maine and New Hampshire were proprietary colonies, settled primarily for profit and advantage. On the other hand, the hopes for economic gains which had led a group of London merchants to plant Virginia and had stimulated a number of British aristocrats to found the Carolinas were not the only inducements to settle in the southern part of the North American continent. Sir George Calvert's wish to find a refuge for English Catholics, William Penn's interest in creating a community in which Quakers could live according to their ideals, Oglethorpe's aim to ameliorate the situation of debt-prisoners—these motives, imbued with humanitarian, religious, and utopian elements, lay behind the foundations of Maryland, Pennsylvania, and Georgia. Although the English promoters of American colonies might have been exclusively interested in the economic aspects of their enterprises, the men whom they persuaded to sail over the ocean and transform the wilderness into a productive land were often those to whom life in Europe had become unbearable and who, perhaps vaguely and almost unconsciously, carried into the New World the dream of a different, of a better, more just social order.

In all regions of the British settlements in North America, one could have found a strong feeling of material realism and a pervasive air of utopian idealism and, consequently, two different attitudes regarding the Old World: attraction and rejection. This does not mean that out of these various elements there slowly emerged a mixture or synthesis which might permit us to speak of a general American view towards England or Europe in the colonial period. This is impossible because of the varying degrees in the original strength which the economic and utopian elements had in each colony; each colony combined them only on a different level. Moreover, the decisive factor which prevents the assumption of a common view of the British colonies in North America, or even of the northern, the middle, or the southern colonies, towards Europe is that such an assumption would be an intellectual construction and have no justification in the reality of the colonial period. Each colony felt itself to be autonomous and independent, a world of its own.

A difficulty in grasping the full extent to which each colony was a separate unit lies in the manner in which charters and grants of the English monarchs, establishing the various colonies, divided up the whole region from latitudes 34° to 45° north. If the geographical data provided in these charters are drawn on a map, the entire North American continent, in a north-south direction from the Bay of Fundy to Cape Hatteras, in an east-west direction through unknown areas to the Pacific Ocean, is distributed among the promoters and founders of plantations. Each grant was contiguous with the territory of the next; in some cases the charters overlapped. The charters and grants, however, described only the areas in which the right to make settlements was given to the owners; they did not expect to populate and cultivate the entire area which had been assigned to them, or even large parts of it. In the first sixty years of English colonization in North America, settlements were restricted to the coast line and extended into the interior only along a few large rivers; the population was thin, and the inhabited areas of each colony seldom stretched along the entire coast line assigned by the charter. The settlements of one colony were usually far removed from the settlements of the next. This situation did not change fundamentally in the second part of the seventeenth century, when wider areas of the interior became settled and cultivated. Open spaces still remained between settlements belonging to different colonies. There was little danger of encroaching on the other's territory; the actual issue was whether single governments were able to control the settlements in the vast areas over which the charters had given authority. Connecticut became an autonomous colony in the area which the Massachusetts Bay Colony claimed. Settlements within the boundaries of the Carolina grant were made chiefly in the southern part; settlements in the northern portion became a separate colony —North Carolina. Nor was it possible to maintain the union which had been established between Pennsylvania and Delaware. Each plantation, set in what to the settlers appeared an infinite wilderness, was confronted by individual tasks created by the particularity of its physical surroundings and the character of the natives. Thus, each colony became accustomed to relying on its own resources and to pursuing its own policy. The colonies might derive their legal existence from the English Crown and to it owe allegiance; but on the American continent, they grew up in their own way.

In 1776, when the colonies became the United States of America and entered the field of foreign policy as an independent power, they had suddenly to assume a function which, previously, England had carried out for them. Yet they were still in the process of accomplishing the necessary preliminary step of developing a consciousness of the community of interest which would set them off as a unit within the state system.

II

In contrast to the colonies, each of which was anxious to chart its own course in the New World, the English government was inclined from the beginning to regard its plantations on the American continent as an entirety. When James I gave the first Virginia charter, he was concerned with the whole area on which Englishmen would settle in the course of the following century. The tendency to deal with the American colonies according to a common policy remained strong in London throughout the period in which the American colonies were part of the British Empire.

This outlook was produced and maintained by political trends, administrative necessities, economic interests, and considerations of power policy. Royal authority was the source of all the enterprises undertaken on American soil. Although the King had little or no part in the organization of the settlements, the Stuart monarchs were concerned about upholding their claims to final authority; and so at appropriate moments, they interfered in the affairs of their colonies. It was no less natural that the special committees and commissions created to handle problems inherent in the existence of colonial possessions—matters of immigration, finance, and defense—would follow a general line and adopt a uniform policy. Furthermore, England's primary interest in her colonies was the regulation of their trade in such a manner that foreigners were excluded and the English merchant would benefit; this led unavoidably to the development of a policy for the colonies as a whole. The trend towards subjecting the colonies to the uniform policy of a central authority in London was not exclusively dependent on the will of the Monarch; therefore, this policy was continued when the absolutist Stuarts had fallen from power. A special committee to determine colonial policy and to enforce it was established by Parliament during the Civil War and the same system for administering the plantations was adopted under the Commonwealth.

These unifying tendencies received a more energetic impulse and a more systematic form after the Restoration of the Stuarts. The changes resulting from this centralizing policy were, however, of short duration on the North American continent. The climax of this policy, the "Dominion of New England," lasted barely three years. The attempt to form one great province, extending from Maine to the Jerseys under one Governor-in-Chief appointed by the King, collapsed with the "glorious revolution." Massachusetts, Connecticut, Rhode Island, New Hampshire, Maine, New York and the Jerseys—which had lost their charters and had been deprived of their legislatures—reemerged as political identities. The administrative changes which Charles II introduced in the colonial bureaucracy in London had lasting significance. All the issues connected with the colonies were placed under a special committee within the Privy Council called the "Lords of Trade and Plantations." Although the particular form of organization devised by the Stuarts did not survive their fall, the centralizing principle which had inspired the establishment of the Lords of Trade and Plantations was adopted and continued by the succeeding rulers.

The "Board of Trade" which was created in 1696 and continued to function throughout the eighteenth century had less power than the Lords of Trade and Plantations which the Board replaced. The former had possessed executive authority, while the Board of Trade had only investigating and advisory functions; it collected information about the colonies and made policy recommendations. Thus, the appointment of colonial officials and the execution of policy were left to traditional office-holders, especially the Secretaries of State. Nevertheless, the existence of an English government agency working steadily and exclusively on colonial affairs was an important factor in producing in London an attitude which opposed colonial particularism in favor of a general imperial interest and which placed colonial affairs within the general framework of English foreign policy.

To the members of the Board of Trade, the struggle against Louis XIV reinforced the need for overcoming colonial independence and for coordinating the policy of the various colonies on the American continent. At the beginning of the War of the Spanish Succession, the Board of Trade complained that these colonies do not take "due care for their own defence and security against an enemy" and maintained "that this chiefly arises from the ill use they make of the powers entrusted to them by their charters and the independency which they pretend to, and that each government is obliged only to defend itself without any consideration had of their neighbours, or of the general preservation of the whole."[4] The great political conflict in which England had become involved not only accentuated the need for a unified imperial policy in London, but also aroused the idea in America that the colonies were tied together by common interests which demanded cooperation and common action. This feeling, however, was by no means general. New York, in the interest of an undisturbed fur trade, refused to take any steps which Canada might regard as provocative and managed to remain neutral during the first half of the War of the Spanish Succession. But New England and South Carolina, which had to bear the brunt of the attack which the allied Bourbon powers of France and Spain directed from the north and from the south against the English possessions in North America, felt that more was involved than their individual fate. South Carolina, so the Governor proclaimed at the time of the outbreak of the war, was "the fronteere Colony of all her Maties Plantations on the Main

---

[4] "Report of the Board of Trade on proprietary governments, March 26, 1701," *English Historical Documents*, vol. IX: *American Colonial Documents*, ed. Merrill Jensen, London 1955, p. 252.

in America."[5] The threat against the North induced the governors of all the colonies above New York to combine their efforts and to agree on a common offensive strategy against the heart of the French possessions, although the inglorious outcome of the campaign against Quebec in 1711 hardly corresponded to the labors which had been necessary to bring about this concerted action. The "particular interests" of each colony began to be opposed to a "national interest" —to use the terms which appear a few years later in a report of the Governor of Pennsylvania.[6]

Although a demand for unified action, evoked by the great war which ushered in the eighteenth century, was voiced in the colonies, this was only a beginning; certainly it was not yet a widespread feeling. It is significant that the protagonists of a joint colonial policy in America were governors, men who were in close contact with the Board of Trade, which was the chief advocate of the necessity of administrative unification. Nor is it accidental that the note of common interest is sounded most emphatically when a colony asked the English government for special assistance to be used in an enterprise which was to the colony's direct and immediate advantage. In 1721, the Board of Trade reported on the "State of the British Plantations in America";[7] speaking of an "Empire in America" from Nova Scotia to South Carolina, it recommended interchange of information and cooperation among the governors of the colonies, the establishment of a common defense system, and, finally, the appointment of a captain general for all the colonies. Certainly

[5] *Journals of the Commons House of Assembly of South Carolina for 1702*, ed. A. S. Salley, Columbia, S.C., 1932, p. 64.

[6] Report by Sir William Keith, February 16, 1719, *Public Record Office*, Colonial Office Papers, C.O. 5:1265, Q 179.

[7] *Documents relative to the Colonial History of the State of New York*, ed. E. B. O'Callaghan, Albany 1855, vol. v, pp. 591-630, especially pp. 623-630.

the authors of this report were far ahead of what was, at this time, the view in the colonies.

In America, a powerful impetus was given to the idea of concerted action and unified policy only in the 1720's and 1730's, the decades following the end of the War of the Spanish Succession. New immigrants, not only from England, but also from Scotland and Ireland, Germany and France, poured over the ocean and extended the regions of settlement beyond the coastal areas into the interior. They began to fill up the land to the Allegheny Mountains and eyed the western lands behind the mountains: the Ohio Valley up to the Great Lakes. But the same rich lands had also attracted the French. In their hands, the region would serve to form a link between Canada and the French settlements of Louisiana. By establishing themselves all along the back of the English possessions, the French would cut off the possibilities of further English expansion; this also would place the French in a formidable strategic position to attack and destroy whatever settlements the English now had on the American continent. In earlier times, only a few were able to discern behind the local skirmishes in America the design of a competition for empire between two great powers; now a wave of British-American patriotism, vilifying the French as "Gens de mauvaise Foy,"[8] swept through the colonies. To many it became evident that the French threat was so formidable that its removal demanded a comprehensive effort. Recognition of the need for concerted action against external enemies was one issue involved in the problems of westward expansion; the other issue was the possibility of clashes between the various colonies of British America because of the lack of an integrated policy and

[8] Max Savelle, "The Appearance of an American Attitude toward External Affairs, 1750-1775," *American Historical Review*, vol. LII (1947), p. 660.

the pursuit of an independent line by each colony. The Ohio Valley, which Maryland, Pennsylvania, and New York regarded as the natural area of settlements for their expanding populations, was claimed by Virginia as its exclusive domain. The period in which the colonies could develop without obstructing each other had passed; their policy would have to be coordinated if they were not to fight with each other.

A consequence of these developments was the famous Albany Plan of 1754. The Albany Congress, called together on the initiative of the Board of Trade, in order to avoid further deterioration in the relations between the English colonies and the Indians, went beyond its original purpose and agreed on a plan for colonial union. It envisaged a government above the individual colonial governments—with a president at its head and a council elected by the assemblies of the colonies. This government would have charge of defense, new settlements, and relations with the Indians; it was to be supported by taxes and customs collected by its own officials. Because this plan left the American federation within the British Empire, it is clear that Britain would have remained responsible for the foreign policy of the united colonies. But by negotiating with the Indians and by acting as a unified power, the colonies would have become aware of their position in the world of foreign affairs. In a slow and gradual manner, they might have been introduced to the problems of foreign policy and made them an issue of reflection and discussion. However, the individual colonies did not support the plan which their commissioners had drafted in Albany. Even at the height of the French threat, the colonies had been hesitant to make any real sacrifice of political independence. For instance, the Maryland Assembly had declared "that the Situation . . . of our Neighbours of Virginia, with regard to any violence or Outrage, threatened or perpetrated against them, by the French, does not require our immediate aid or Assistance, by the raising of an armed Force here . . . ."[9] Thus, it was perhaps natural that such a radical departure from the traditions of colonial autonomy and independence as the Albany Plan represented was not immediately approved. Then the outcome of the Seven Years' War so completely changed the situation which had produced the Albany Plan that the validity of its ideas was not even subjected to any further examination. With the English conquest of Canada, the French lost power over the north; the threat which had prompted the need for concerted action had disappeared. No further progress was achieved towards a unified attitude in foreign affairs in the period between the end of the Seven Years' War and the American Revolution. The colonies had not become conscious of themselves as a political unit distinct from other political units; they had no practical experience with a unified policy in foreign affairs; and they had not given any systematic thought to the issues involved in the management of diplomacy when they entered the field of foreign policy.

III

It was to Europe that the American leaders in 1776 had to turn for instruction about the traditions and nature of diplomacy. Eighteenth-century America did not lack information about the European political scene. Connections between the Old World and the New World had improved: sailings had become faster and more regular. A continuously swelling stream of new immigrants provided knowledge about recent events in various parts of Europe. With the growth in population and the rise of important commercial cities along the coast from Boston to Charlestown, social life had become more complex; professional men, lawyers and doctors, took their place in a society previously domi-

[9] *Ibid.*, p. 657.

nated by ministers, merchants, and planters. To serve the needs for greater intellectual refinement, printing shops and newspapers were founded; the literary products of the European Enlightenment became well-known, so that America and Europe were joined in an intellectual community. Yet the adoption and acceptance of European ideas, at least in the field of foreign policy, was selective and creative rather than purely imitative. Although the experience of the colonies as members of the British Empire had not wrought an approach to foreign policy which the independent republic could use, the colonial period had produced certain fundamental assumptions which made the Americans particularly receptive to those European notions which corresponded to them. The process by which these two elements—European notions and American assumptions—were developed into a special American approach to foreign policy is the topic of this book.

As we have said, the most important motives which led Englishmen to seek a new future on the North American continent were material advantages and utopian hopes. The Americans entered the field of foreign affairs with assumptions deriving from these motives.

A reflection of the economic motive can be seen in the close connection which, in American eyes, existed between commerce and foreign policy. Of course, it was natural for people whose main contacts with the outside world were those of trade and commerce to regard these activities as the principal object of foreign relations. Moreover, this tendency was reinforced by the mercantilist policy which England had pursued and in consequence of which the colonies were cut off from trade contacts with other nations. Thus, the existence or non-existence of commercial relations with other powers appeared as the touchstone of participation in a state system as an independent power.

The utopian hopes which immigrants had connected with their settlement in America made it difficult for them to fit themselves meekly into the existing state system and to become a power like all other powers. Americans expected that the appearance of their country on the diplomatic scene would be instrumental in effecting a new departure in international relations and would usher in a new and better world. Americans would be inclined to listen to those voices which were critical of the existing methods of foreign policy and wanted to reform them rather than to accept them as appropriate and necessary.

But in addition to these preconceptions which gave a special direction to American thinking on foreign affairs, the entire colonial experience made foreign policy particularly alien and repulsive to Americans. It was difficult for them to comprehend the importance of the power factor in foreign relations. In Europe, international agreements legalized situations which were brought about by a clash of opposing powers. Treaties could not and did not pretend to reestablish an original situation of law and rights, which, in the changes and developments of a history extending over more than a thousand years, had become undistinguishable, if it had ever existed. On the North American continent, law and power were sharply contrasted, irreconcilable with each other. The settlers had come to America with their charters and grants establishing their right; the validity of their claims against those who inhabited this continent before the English came could be maintained only by assuming that the Indians lived in a pre-social world, devoid of rights. If the Indians resisted and a struggle ensued, this was not a fight of equal power against equal power, still less a fight of right against right. A social order began only when the chaos of the pre-social anarchy had been overcome, when right was established. The world of Law began when the world of Power had ended. Certainly, one should not emphasize exclusively the colonial experience in explaining the role which the idea of law played in American political thinking. There were other influences in American eighteenth-century thought which worked in the same direction: the strongly legalistic tradition of English political life and the importance, for America, of the problems of navigation which, in the seventeenth century, had provided a decisive impetus for the codification of a law of nations. The strength of the American belief in the impossibility of transforming Power into Right is an important fact; it increased the complexity of the task with which the Americans were faced in 1776: finding their way in a world of power politics.

CHAPTER II

Insula Fortunata:

THE ENGLISH PATTERN FOR AMERICAN
FOREIGN POLICY

I

WHEN the Americans were faced with the necessity of forming a system of foreign policy, they looked to England for a pattern of what their attitude ought to be.

The American Revolution was directed against an English government which had become tyrannical and against a monarch who was a despot, but it was not a revolt against English political ideas. On the contrary, the Americans believed that in taking up arms they were defending the true rights of Englishmen and they acted as legitimate heirs of the proud English tradition of freedom, handed on in an unbroken succession from the days of Magna Carta. Although they were fighting against the English, the Americans could have no compunctions about using English political experiences for the construction of their new political life.

Moreover, England offered the unique example of a country in which foreign policy was an object of public debate. On the European Continent, absolutism stifled public political discussion; foreign affairs especially were considered as an arcanum—managed and understood only by the monarch and a few nobles. In England, the Whigs, as the protagonists and beneficiaries of the "glorious revolution" and bound to its traditions, had an interest in airing political issues in Parliament and in gaining the support of public opinion. Debates in Parliament were secret then; but speeches of parliamentary leaders were frequently published anonymously, and all political problems of significance were discussed extensively in numerous pamphlets.

Finally, there was a special reason why a lively, almost passionate debate on foreign affairs took place in England during the eighteenth century in the period between the Peace of Utrecht and the American Revolution. During these six decades, the European state system underwent an almost complete transformation, and England's role in European power politics, particularly, was decisively changed. Since the beginning of the sixteenth century, when the contest for the possession of Italy had covered Europe with a network of antagonisms and alliances, European diplomacy had been dominated by the rivalry of two great dynasties, the Bourbon and the Hapsburg. The center of action had been mainly in Central and Southern Europe. England had been more a spectator than a participant in the conflict; her interest had been to prevent the Continental supremacy of one power or a universal monarchy which would have endangered England's security and independence. The War of the Spanish Succession was the last great struggle between the houses of Bourbon and Hapsburg. The active and leading role which England had played in this war to thwart Louis XIV's bid for hegemony was indicative of the change which was taking place in European foreign politics. Financial power and economic strength had proved to be a determining factor; trading privileges and colonial possessions, which constituted the most important sources of the wealth of a state, came to be primary objects in the contests of the European powers. Consequently, the political center of gravity shifted from Southern and Central Europe to the Atlantic seaboard; and the weight of England in the European state system was increased. The significance of the Franco-Austrian hostility paled in comparison with the importance of the Anglo-French "competition for empire." In the place of the Bourbons and Hapsburgs, England and France emerged as the principal rivals on the European political scene.

Austria, excluded from direct access to the ocean and to the new sources of wealth, tried to replace this relative loss of strength by embarking on a new policy; she turned to the southeast, building an empire in the Danube Valley and in the Balkans, and was drawn into the new orbit of Eastern European politics. This is the century of the appearance of Russia in the politics of Europe and of the rise of Prussia, which, by its territorial expansion, bridged the previously separated eastern and western halves of Europe. The gradual disappearance of the Continental conflicts between France and Austria, the vehemence of the Anglo-French colonial rivalry, and the incorporation of Russia and Prussia within the European system were events that made the eighteenth century a landmark in the history of European diplomacy. It was the great achievement of the elder Pitt that he perceived this rise of a new political constellation in Europe and firmly adapted England's foreign policy to the new situation. In planning the course of English foreign policy, he placed commercial and colonial aims above all others. Oceans and colonies should be the decisive scene of action. England's relations to the European Continent became of secondary importance and had to be subordinated to these new aims. The main task of England's European policy was to restrict France, which alone could endanger Britain's colonial empire, to the Continent and to keep France from employing her forces overseas. With Austria gradually losing interest in Western Europe, Prussia was to take Austria's place as England's ally in checking France.

Such a reorientation may appear to us as a logical step, a

necessary adjustment to a new situation. But to contemporaries, this change in alliances and strategy appeared to be a radical departure from tradition; a forceful and self-assured leader like Pitt was needed to carry through this realignment, which was preceded by many years of uncertain groping and wavering. Since the accession of the Hanoverian dynasty in 1715, England was ruled by the Whigs. They had come to power with a definite set of ideas on foreign policy, formed in their long struggles against the Tories. In the view of King George I and of his ministers, the "strange notion" "that England can subsist by itself, whatever becomes of the rest of Europe" was "butt the old Tory one" "which has been so justly exploded by the Whigs, ever since the Revolution."[1] The Whigs claimed that England's safety was dependent on the maintenance of a balance of power on the European Continent. England, therefore, must take an active part in the diplomatic movements and the wars of the Continent. Yet, since the Whigs controlled English policy just when the foundation of European diplomacy began to shift, the Whigs themselves became doubtful of the wisdom of a rigid adherence to their old principles. They split into various groups, recommending various courses of action. The differences of opinion which once had formed the dividing line between Whigs and Tories now became sources of discord among the Whigs themselves. It was said of Robert Walpole, the Whig Prime Minister, that he adopted the foreign policy of the Tories for the Whig party. He proclaimed: "My politics are to keep free from all engagements as long as we possibly can"[2]; and once he emphasized in the House of Commons:

[1] Lord Sunderland to Lord Townshend, November 11, 1716, *Historical Manuscripts Commission, Eleventh Report*, Appendix, Part IV: The Manuscripts of the Marquess Townshend, London 1887, p. 103.

[2] Walpole to Lord Townshend, July/August 1723, see William Coxe, *Memoirs of the Life and Administration of Sir Robert Walpole*, vol. II, London 1798, p. 263.

"This is a trading nation, and the prosperity of her trade is what ought to be principally in the eye of every gentleman in this House."[3] Preservation of peace, the presupposition of a flourishing trade, became Walpole's primary goal. He always used England's influence on the Continent to remove possible causes of friction and to reconcile conflicts. Walpole saw, as his critics complained, the foremost interest of British foreign policy lying not in the maintenance of the balance of power, but "in the tranquility of Europe"[4]; and thereby he clearly deviated from the traditional "meddling" policy of the Whigs. In contrast to Walpole, his successor, Carteret, who guided English foreign policy in the War of the Austrian Succession, returned to the "old system" of the Whigs. He considered it his task to "knock the heads of the Kings of Europe together" and "to make Kings and Emperors."[5] Under the pretense of the maintenance of the balance of power, he gave free rein to his inclination to pile up alliances and accumulate treaties.

Thus the time between the two great world wars of the eighteenth century—the War of the Spanish Succession and the Seven Years' War—was a period of uncertainty in British foreign policy, characterized by frequent shifting of alliances, zigzag diplomacy, and sudden diplomatic revolutions. When Pitt, the great realist, ended this wavering between the divergent lines of policy, he united the opposing systems, taking from each what seemed useful. He acknowledged England's interest in the affairs of the Continent, but he subordinated it to the strengthening of England as a maritime and trading power.

[3] In House of Commons, March 8, 1739, see Cobbett's *Parliamentary History of England*, vol. x, p. 1291.

[4] Bathurst on Walpole in House of Lords, February 13, 1741, see *Parliamentary History of England*, vol. xi, p. 1142.

[5] Basil Williams, *Carteret and Newcastle. A Contrast in Contemporaries*, Cambridge 1943, p. 2.

The fluid diplomatic situation formed the background for the vehement public discussion on foreign affairs extending throughout this entire period. The great number of pamphlets which were concerned with issues of foreign policy is indicative of misgivings about the course which the government pursued and of widespread feelings of uncertainty about the position which England ought to take in the European conflicts. The battle of the pamphlets started along the traditional lines of the seventeenth-century struggle between Whigs and Tories. There were those who stood for England's interest in the preservation of the balance of power; and there were others who emphasized the advantages of England's insular position, characterizing the attitude of their opponents as "Quixotism" and as an attempt to "revive those Ages of Knight Errantry."[6] It was asked "whether it might be more conducive to the true interest of this nation, to rely wholly upon that situation which disjoins it from the rest of the world, to encrease its naval force, and to give its great application to the marine without concerning itself with the intrigues of the neighbouring states; or once more to cover Flanders with our troops, to negotiate, to fight, and to expend our treasure, in restraining the overgrown power of France, and in preserving the balance of power in Europe."[7]

The fundamental question of whether England had to take an active part in the struggles for maintaining a European balance of power or whether she could remain a disinterested spectator was enlivened by current and practical political issues. One new problem introduced in the discussion derived from the accession of the Hanoverian

[6] *Considerations offered upon the approaching peace and upon the importance of Gibraltar to the British Empire, Being the second Part of the Independent Whig,* London 1720.

[7] *The Important Question discussed or, a Serious and Impartial Enquiry into the Interest of England with respect to the continent,* London 1746.

dynasty to the English throne. The Act of Settlement contained the provision that "in case the Crown and Imperial dignity of this Realm shall hereafter come to any person not being a native of this Kingdom of England, this nation shall not be obliged to engage in any war for the defence of any dominions or territories, which do not belong to the Crown of England, without the consent of Parliament." Thus the debate on foreign policy became tied up with a critical domestic issue. If it could be shown that English participation in the wars of Europe merely benefitted the interest of the Hanoverian dynasty in enhancing the glory of its Continental dominion, this could be used to place further restrictions on the freedom of action of the monarch and to strengthen the position of Parliament in its relations with the Crown. The popular preoccupation with this question, whether or not the Hanoverian Continental commitments deflected English foreign policy from its proper course, may be deduced from the outspoken titles of some pamphlets: Was "the interest of Great Britain steadily pursued," or was "the interest of Hanover steadily pursued"?[8] This controversy became particularly heated when, in the 1740's after Walpole's fall, Carteret resumed a policy of active English intervention in Continental affairs. Pitt, then still a young man and lacking the balanced judgment on foreign affairs which he achieved in later years, spoke bitter words in the House of Commons: "This great, this powerful, this formidable kingdom, is considered only as a province to a despicable electorate,"[9] words that were echoed frequently in the pamphlets of the period. The most trenchant formulation can be found in a pamphlet by Chesterfield: "The whole

[8] *The interest of Hanover steadily pursued being a Sequel to a late Pamphlet, Intitled, The Interest of Great Britain Steadily pursued*, London 1743.

[9] December 10, 1742, see *Parliamentary History of England*, vol. XII, p. 1035.

strength of the British empire was to be steer'd by the
Hanover Rudder."[10] Chesterfield was convinced that Carteret, with his numerous treaties of subsidies and alliances,
had exceeded the limits of a sound British foreign policy;
yet Chesterfield did not take the extreme stand that England
had no interest in the Continent at all or that the balance of
power was a mere chimera. He tried to devise a definitive
rule for England's relation with the Continent. Chesterfield
felt that England ought to have "laid it down as an invari-
able Maxim, never to enter into a Land-War, never, but
when the Dutch Barrier was in Danger. . . ." Chesterfield's
rich experience in active politics may have taught him to shy
away from the extremes and to look for a middle position.
Another practical statesman, Bolingbroke, who, in the
Patriot King, provided a systematic discussion of the guiding
principles of English foreign policy, made a similar mediating
recommendation: "As we cannot be easily nor suddenly
attacked, and as we ought not to aim at any acquisition of
territory on the continent, it may be our interest to watch
the secret workings of the several councils abroad; to advise
and warn; to abet and oppose; but it never can be our true
interest easily and officiously to enter into action, much less
into engagements that imply action and expense. . . . This
is the post of advantage and honour, which our singular
situation among the powers of Europe determines us, or
should determine us, to take, in all disputes that happen on
the continent. . . . By a continual attention to improve her
natural, that is her maritime strength, by collecting all her
forces within herself, and reserving them to be laid out on
great occasions, such as regard her immediate interests and
her honour, or such as are truly important to the general

[10] *The case of the Hanover forces in the pay of Great Britain impartially and freely examined with some seasonable reflections on the
present conjuncture of affairs*, London 1743.

system of power in Europe; she may be the arbitrator of differences, the guardian of liberty, and the preserver of that balance, which has been so much talked of, and is so little understood. . . ."[11]

If the occupation of the English throne by princes who were also rulers of a German state brought a new element into the controversy over England's role in European conflicts, the debate was further enlivened by the increasing importance which the trading community had gained in eighteenth-century England. It was argued that English economic interests might best be served by abstention from European conflicts. It was said by those who stressed England's indifference to the affairs of the Continent that trade was England's main interest and that "a trading nation should avoid a war if possible."[12] Among those who advocated the subordination of English foreign policy to commercial interests, there were a number of writers who were thorough pacifists; in their opinion, England's insular position permitted her to abandon all power politics. Their motto could be found in a pamphlet ascribed to Lord Hervey: "From a Warlike Genius, and an Enterprizing Minister, Good Lord deliver us."[13] England was in no need of bellicose statesmanship; for "Nature has separated us from the continent . . . and as no man ought to endeavour to separate whom God Almighty has joined, so no man ought to endeavour to join what God Almighty has separated."[14] Peace served the trading interests better than any other

---

[11] This passage from Bolingbroke's *Patriot King* is reprinted in *English Historical Documents*, vol. x: *1714-1783*, ed. D. B. Horn and Mary Ransom, London 1957, pp. 845-846.

[12] *The Treaty of Seville and the measures that have been taken for the four last years, impartially considered*, London 1730.

[13] *Miscellaneous Thoughts on the present Posture of our foreign and Domestic Affairs*, London 1742.

[14] The Earl of Pomfret in the House of Lords, December 10, 1755, see *Parliamentary History of England*, vol. xv, p. 653.

policy. Admittedly, England had a strong interest in inter-course with other powers because of her commerce: "Treaties of commerce are Bonds that we ought to contract with our Neighbors"; yet as to the nature of such bonds, the same author stated that a trading nation "ought not to con-cern itself with particular nations, or Schemes of Govern-ment in distant countries . . . her interest requires that she should live if possible in constant Harmony with all Nations, that she may better enjoy the Effects of their friendship in the Benefits resulting from their Commerce."[15] Another writer[16] assumed that Britain could be sure of being left in peace because of the interest of other nations in continuing trade with her. Still another pamphleteer stated that all treaties of Great Britain with the various powers of Europe have not "produced any advantage to us."[17] Therefore, he drew up a general rule: "A Prince or State ought to avoid all Treaties, except such as tend towards promoting Commerce or Manufactures . . . . All other Alliances may be look'd upon as so many Incumbrances." The pamphlets of this pacifist group represented the most radical position in the discussion on the aims and means of English foreign policy during the eighteenth century.

Although the basic issues were the same which had divid-ed Whigs and Tories in the seventeenth century—namely, involvement in Europe for the purposes of the maintenance of a balance of power, versus advantages of insular position —the public debate of the eighteenth century clarified the implications of the two contrary points of view. In particular, the possibility of refraining from European alliances and

[15] *A Modest Enquiry into the Present State of Foreign Affairs*, Lon-don [1742].

[16] *A Detection of the Views of those who would in the present Crisis, engage an incumber'd, Trading Nation, as Principals, in a ruinous expensive Land-War; in answer to a Pamphlet: The important Question*, London 1746.

[17] *Political Maxims by Phil. Anglus*, London 1744.

conflicts appeared in a new light. Originally such an attitude had been advocated for the negative reason that as long as England possessed a powerful fleet, her insular position provided safety against external attack. Now this policy received a positive meaning: it permitted concentration on expansion overseas and served to maintain and increase economic prosperity. It is no wonder that the idea of such a policy was frequently felt to be something entirely new. As one of the pamphlets said, the idea of keeping away from Continental wars "never entered into any Man's Heart till of late Years."[18] What, asked the Dutch diplomat Count Bentinck with astonishment in 1745, would the English statesmen of the last century, should they be alive, think, if they "had heard an English Nobleman say that it signify as little who is Emperor, as who is Lord Mayor of London"?[19] Bentinck also mentioned that he had heard in London drawing rooms a new term used to characterize this policy of keeping away from the Continent: "des principes isolés."[20] This aspect of English thinking on foreign affairs was also known on the Continent; a French handbook on European politics explicitly referred to the new English trend "à rompre ce qu'elle appelle Continental Connections, ou liaisons avec le Continent."[21]

The public debate was not silenced when, in the 1750's, Pitt set English foreign policy and strategy on a new course. The question of the war aims—whether acquisition of Canada or of the economically valuable French islands in the West Indies was more advantageous to England—excited

[18] *The important Questions concerning Invasions, a Sea War, Raising the militia and paying subsidies for Foreign Troops*, London 1755.
[19] William Bentinck to the Countess of Portland, September 7, 1745, *Briefwisseling en Aanteekeningen van Willem Bentinck, Heer van Rhoon*, ed. C. Gerretson and P. Geyl, vol. I, Utrecht 1934, p. 139.
[20] *Ibid.*, p. 131.
[21] de Peyssonel, *Situation Politique de la France et ses rapports actuels avec toutes les Puissances de l'Europe*, n.p. 1789, p. 238.

public opinion. However, as long as the French were contesting the English expansion in America, Pitt could pursue his dual policy of colonial aggrandizement on the one hand and of a Continental alliance with Prussia on the other without much opposition. No one dared to charge Pitt with un-English and Hanoverian sympathies; constitutional bickering disappeared from the debate. One pamphleteer stated frankly that he had been "no friend to Continental Measures in general" and that he was especially opposed to "such continental measures as engaged us during the three last Wars, as Principals . . . . But the Continental measures now adopted by England were necessary, both with Regard to our Honor and Our Interest."[22] Yet when, after the defeat of the French in Canada, Pitt stuck to the Prussian alliance and a continuation of the war, the debate about foreign policy was taken up with renewed vigor. In 1761, one of the most famous English pamphlets of the eighteenth century appeared: Israel Mauduit's *Considerations on the Present German War*. This pamphlet is said to have caused Pitt's downfall, having had "more operation in working a change on the minds of men than perhaps ever fell to the lot of a pamphlet."[23]

Mauduit did more than marshal the outworn arguments. He tried to discover the reality behind the concepts used in the controversy; his pamphlet culminated in an analysis of the term "Continental connections." He showed that this term had one meaning when applied to the War of the Spanish Succession and another meaning when used to describe England's policy toward the Continent in his own time. In the War of the Spanish Succession, the whole Continent had been united against France; England had been just one

[22] *A Letter, Addressed to Two great Men on the Prospect of Peace*, London 1760.

[23] Horace Walpole on Mauduit, as quoted in the article "Israel Mauduit," *Dictionary of National Biography*.

member of a large coalition. In Mauduit's time, England was allied only to a few secondary powers like Prussia, Hanover, and Brunswick.

The present alliances served much more limited objectives than the participation in the Great Coalition. During the War of the Spanish Succession, general European interests like the defense of the freedom of Protestantism or prevention of a universal monarchy had required England's interference in Continental politics; these aims had been achieved. In Mauduit's time, connections with Continental powers could have only the purpose of promoting English national interests—the expansion of the empire. But Mauduit did not believe that Continental alliances were necessary for this purpose, not even financial subsidies to German states. On the contrary, they were detrimental to the English interests, for they kept alive disunity among the German states. Without British interference, one power would get the upper hand and unify Germany. A united Germany would then form a perfect counterweight against France. Thus, if England left the Continent to itself, she could ultimately benefit by the creation of a balance of power, the perennial panacea of British diplomacy. There was a mixture of falsehood and truth in Mauduit's reasoning. In his time, a united Germany was a utopia; Mauduit also failed to see that even a disunited Germany neutralized an important part of the French forces. But he assumed correctly that the aims of the British and their allies in the War of the Spanish Succession were fundamentally different from those which Pitt pursued when he allied England with Prussia in the Seven Years' War. Now England's chief interest in the Continent was to have the European powers so interlocked with each other that England would have a free hand in the other parts of the globe. It may be doubted that Mauduit was right in believing that this aim could be achieved without the active interference of

England in European politics. But in propounding this thesis, Mauduit reinforced powerfully the arguments which previous writers had raised against "Continental connections"; he provided the best reasoned recommendation of a policy of isolation.

The practical political importance of the "battle of the pamphlets" should not be overestimated. Probably the mighty Whig families were not swayed one way or another by the arguments of the scribblers. Reared on their country estates and drawing their strength from their ruling position in their counties, with the self-assurance of a class traditionally accustomed to wielding power, they relied more on their instinct than on technical knowledge, more on an imperturbable confidence in their ability to handle emergencies as they arose than on any capacity to prevent them by foresight. Yet they had come to power as the protagonists of Parliament and People against the Crown; and, even under the Hanoverian dynasty which they themselves had established, the contest between King and Parliament was a living issue. Thus they needed to keep contact with public opinion and to make sure of its continued support. The emphasis on the dangers of the Hanoverian influence in English foreign policy might be partly explained by the particular effectiveness of this argument in arousing the distrust of the public against the court. The stress on the trading interests of England may be linked with the special position of the merchants in English political life; they were a small, yet an independent and influential group which could make its voice heard and, if necessary, turn the scales of a decision at a critical moment.

Thus in England, foreign policy had lost the character of a "secret science" which only a few initiated could handle. It aroused the interest of wide groups of society and was an important element in the formation of "public opinion."

II

The contents of the public debate on foreign affairs which was conducted in England during the eighteenth century could become known in America in three ways. Americans could absorb the ideas of this discussion while they were travelling in England or residing some time there for business reasons. Books and tracts, brought over from England, or American reprints of English publications might provide this information. Finally, Englishmen who came to America might divulge the views which had been aired in England.

All three channels of communication served to spread in America knowledge of recent English thinking on foreign affairs.

Quite a considerable number of the colonists knew England through personal experience, from a relatively short stay, or from a residence extending over several years. There were the Colonial Agents, who were in steady contact with the Board of Trade and members of Parliament; and there were also the colonial merchants, who had dealings with London bankers and importers. A voyage to Europe and a stay in England were frequently regarded as necessary to perfect the education of a young gentleman. Sons of plantation-owners in the southern colonies were often sent out on the "grand tour" before they settled on their estates in South Carolina or Virginia. Many young men went to England for their professional training; among those who later played a prominent role in the American Revolution, Charles Carroll, Charles Cotesworth Pinckney, Jacob Rush, and Arthur Lee had read law at the Inner and Middle Temple; and Benjamin Rush had studied medicine at the University of Edinburgh and served an apprenticeship in London hospitals. It was natural that, in the years of growing tension between the colonies and England which preceded the outbreak of the armed conflict, Americans abroad tended to associate with those English people who favored the American cause. Americans became acquainted with Whig radicals who included in their general program of political reform the demand for a new departure in foreign policy. There was also a practical reason why American visitors in England moved particularly among men of advanced political views; they formed the circle of Benjamin Franklin, to whom, as the one American with a great reputation in Europe, Americans turned for introductions into English society. Franklin had an intimate knowledge of the English discussion on foreign policy. He himself had participated in the debate over the war aims during the Seven Years' War. In two pamphlets, in which he had revealed himself as a follower of Pitt, he had called attention to the great value of Canada, in order to prevent the exchange of Canada for Guadeloupe. At the same time, however, he had attacked the pamphleteers who demanded immediate peace. In those years, Franklin had demonstrated little inclination towards innovation in foreign policy. Since his main concern had been territorial expansion and security against attack, he had placed the interests of power politics over those of economics. But notes which he jotted down some years later show that he had become well acquainted with the arguments of those who criticized conventional diplomacy. Then he spoke disparagingly of the "whims about the balance of power," of the "English European quarrels," and of "continental connexions."[24]

But a stay in England was not necessary to become informed about these trends of thought. The extent to which a careful student of political literature could familiarize himself with them in America can be illustrated with the example

[24] Benjamin Franklin, *Works*, ed. Jared Sparks, vol. IV, Philadelphia 1840, pp. 291, 292.

of John Adams. As a young man, he read several writings of Bolingbroke. In view of Adam's future revolutionary career, it is not without amusement that we learn about the great satisfaction he felt with George III's first speech to Parliament which proved him worthy of the title of a "Patriot King."[25] Since the *Patriot King* contained an extensive discussion of English foreign policy, Bolingbroke's opinions on this subject must have been known to Adams. Adams was also well acquainted with Israel Mauduit's *Considerations on the Present German War*,[26] which had made a great impression in Massachusetts; Israel Mauduit and his brother Jasper owed their elections as agents of the colony to the fame of this pamphlet. Significant also is Adams' interest in the *Political Disquisitions* by James Burgh. This book has been characterized as the "Bible" of the Whigs[27]; all tenets of British eighteenth-century progressivism were set forth in the book, including a program of foreign policy. Burgh emphasized that the people were the "fountain of all authority and government." He demanded a more adequate representation of the people in Parliament, and he attacked both court influence and parliamentary corruption; he also denounced a standing army and spoke in favor of a militia. Burgh was a pacifist who considered war "the peculiar disgrace of human nature" and who thought it wiser to "keep clear of quarrels among other states." Since the times of Queen Anne, England unfortunately had "attached herself to continental schemes." There was no reason "to intangle ourselves with the disputes between the powers of the continent"; "Continental connections" had only "ruinous

[25] John Adams, *Works*, ed. Charles Francis Adams, vol. II, Boston 1850, p. 118, also pp. 23, 24.
[26] *Ibid.*, p. 141.
[27] See the article "James Burgh," *Dictionary of National Biography*. The following quotations from James Burgh, *Political Disquisitions*, Philadelphia 1775, can be found in vol. I, pp. xxii, xxiii; vol. II, pp. 341, 388; vol. III, p. 288.

effects." Adams went so far in his enthusiasm about this book that he "contributed somewhat to make the *Disquisitions* more known and attended to in several parts of America."[28] Adams seems to have been successful. Burgh's book was frequently quoted in newspapers; the list of subscribers to its first American edition in 1775 contained names of leading colonists such as Washington, Jefferson, Bowdoin, Hancock, and others. For a time, Burgh's *Political Disquisitions* achieved the position of a minor classic in America. The popularity of the book in the colonies is an indication that at least the fundamental outlines of the debate on the advantages and disadvantages of "Continental connections" were known in America at the time of the first Continental Congress.

Information about the debate on foreign policy could also have come from recent English immigrants to America. Of this, there is such a famous example that all further question whether ideas of this discussion were known in the colonies becomes superfluous. For by one stroke, the English controversy on foreign policy and Continental connections was transferred to the colonies on the eve of independence by Thomas Paine in his famous pamphlet *Common Sense.*

At first glance, it may seem surprising to connect Paine's words with the political controversy which had developed in England, for they seem the hurried product of an emergency situation peculiar to the colonies, written to press a few timely political demands like that of declaring independence. A closer study, however, will show that these practical political recommendations form only a part of a skillfully organized whole. The pamphlet contains two parts. In the first section, a few general considerations on the difference between society and government and on the purposes of gov-

[28] John Adams to James Burgh, December 28, 1774, printed in John Adams, *Works*, vol. IX, p. 351.

ernment led Paine to a thesis which was novel and revolutionary in the age of Montesquieu and Blackstone. Paine maintained that the English constitution was not perfect, that, on the contrary, it was a most unsatisfactory instrument of government. In justification of this unusual statement, he argued that a "simple thing" is better than a "complex thing"; the mixed nature of the English constitution, with its monarchical, aristocratic, and republican elements and its complicated system of checks and balances, was proof of its imperfection. He implemented this criticism by a detailed discussion of the faults of any monarchical constitution, and the first section ended with the statement that monarchy can never be an ideal system of government. This first part was mainly critical in character; yet through this negative attitude, it revealed what Paine considered the ideal form of government—a republic, in which all power emanates from the people.

In the second part, Paine plunged rather suddenly into the discussion of the "state of American affairs" and advised a constructive program for a policy of the New World. Yet there is a significant connection between the two sections: the constructive program of the second part is the logical sequence of Paine's criticism of the European monarchies in the first part. Because the English constitution was faulty, and because Europe was unable to achieve a perfect constitution, it was the duty of America to break with Europe, to make use of her unique opportunities, and to realize the ideal republic. Paine proclaimed that now the propitious moment for the separation from the Old World had come, that America had all the means necessary to achieve independence. Just because Europe had failed, it was America's responsibility to fulfill her own political tasks. This grandiose plea culminated in the brief outline of the future constitution of America.

If we analyze the various threads out of which the fabric of *Common Sense* is woven, the fibre of American political and social conditions seems to predominate. Unquestionably, Paine tried to enliven his work with local coloring. He illustrated the danger of being tied to England's "rotten constitution" by a reference to the severe moral customs of New England, according to which "a man who is attached to a prostitute is unfitted to choose or judge a wife." The familiar theme in eighteenth-century political literature of the emergence of society and government from the state of nature reads like a new story as told by Paine in the light of American frontier conditions. When, in describing the origins of government, he wrote about the "convenient tree" "under the branches of which the whole colony may assemble to deliberate on public matters" and which will serve as the first state house, we are reminded of the first representative assembly in America convening on wooded Jamestown Island and of the Pilgrims taking their first steps towards an organization of social life in their new home.

Still more strongly, *Common Sense* bears the imprint of the tense political situation which had developed in Philadelphia during the latter part of the year 1775 when Paine was writing his pamphlet. Robert Livingston characterized the situation well when he said, "We are between hawk and buzzard; we puzzle ourselves between the commercial and warlike opposition."[29] In the first Continental Congress of 1774, the Moderates, who wanted to remain within the British Empire, had given in to the Radicals, who aimed at independence; all trade, export, and import with England had been prohibited. The Moderates had hoped that a purely commercial opposition would avoid a complete break with Britain and leave the door open for further negotiations; the Radicals

[29] October 6, 1775, see *Journals of the Continental Congress*, ed. Worthington Chauncey Ford, vol. iii, Washington 1905, p. 484.

did not press further, because they were well aware that the people were not yet ready for independence. But when the second Continental Congress convened in 1775, relations between England and the colonies had deteriorated; it had become clear that it was impossible to remain in a halfway position: the alternative was to retreat or to advance. Force had been used at Lexington and Concord. England had successfully withstood the pressure of the American commercial boycott, but the economic situation in the colonies had become critical. To the Radicals, a straight course towards independence seemed to be the only solution. In July 1775, Franklin proposed "articles of confederation" which were designed to give the Congress full power over war and peace. John Adams concerned himself with plans for the creation of a navy. The touchiest question was the problem of trade. In October 1775, a motion was made for the "opening of ports." The ensuing debate on the "state of trade" demonstrated the complexity of this issue.[30] Some held to the hope that America could exist without commerce, but most seemed to regard such an idea as wishful thinking rather than a realistic policy. But every other decision was full of risks and dangers. "If we drop our commercial system of opposition," it was said, "we are undone; we must fail." On the other hand, English seapower would make it impossible for American merchant ships to reach foreign ports without protection by a foreign navy. But if America applied for assistance to France and Spain, then the break with England would be final. "When you once offer your trade to foreign nations, away with all hopes of reconciliation." The Congress could not come to any decision in this dilemma. The Radicals attained some small successes: the Congress authorized the construction of a navy, and a Committee of Secret Corre-

[30] *Ibid.*, pp. 476-504; the following quotations can be found on pp. 479, 498.

spondence was formed which was to undertake some cautious exploration of the attitude of foreign powers to the American cause. But no decision was made on the most urgent and important issues: on confederation, on the opening of ports, or on foreign assistance. Most of all, the majority of the Congress, in accord with the feeling of the people, still shied away from voicing "this dreadful, this alarming sound" of the word "independence."[31] At the end of the year 1776, the sentiment among the Radicals was one of embitterment and frustration.

This was the state of affairs when Paine composed *Common Sense*. The practical demands of this pamphlet suggest that he knew well what had happened behind the closed doors of the Continental Congress. All the arguments of the Radicals in the fall and winter of 1775 were summarized in Paine's pamphlet. He spoke disparagingly of continuing petitions to the King, advocated the building of an American navy, urged the immediate formation of a confederation, stressed the importance of foreign assistance, and advised opening the ports. The culmination of Paine's treatise, the first public call for independence, was only the logical corollary of these postulates. It was as though Paine had been asked by the Radicals to set their program before the public.

So much for the American background of *Common Sense*. As we have seen, Paine's pamphlet argued that the foundation of an independent America was necessary not only for reasons of political expediency but also as the fulfillment of a duty to mankind. The demands for an independent America were embedded in a general social philosophy which can clearly be traced to trends of political thought which were current in England whence Paine had come to the colonies only two years before.

[31] "To the people of Pennsylvania," October 11, 1775, see *American Archives*, ed. Peter Force, fourth series, vol. III, Washington 1840, p. 1013.

When discoursing on the defects of monarchies, Paine re-
told a well-known Biblical story: Samuel announced to the
Jews that they had provoked the ire of God by begging for a
king, and he forewarned them of the sufferings they would
have to bear under a monarchy. This chapter of the Bible is
famous in the history of political thought. A stumbling block
to the political theorists of the Middle Ages who believed in
the monarchy as the ideal form of government, it was popular with all thinkers of republican convictions. Milton used it
extensively in his *Defensio pro populo Anglicano;* so, too,
did Algernon Sidney in his *Discourses on Government.* By
alluding to the same story, Paine revealed himself a true follower of the great republican tradition in English political
thought.

Paine was also influenced by those writers who were the
representatives of this tradition in his own time. In particular, there is a close relation between Paine's ideas in *Common
Sense* and those of Joseph Priestley in his *Essay on the First
Principles of Government* which had been published in 1771.
Paine and Priestley shared fundamental political beliefs;
both claimed that the people should enjoy as much liberty as
possible and should have complete political power. Priestley
had not openly attacked the monarchical system of government; yet he had expressed some doubts about the wisdom of
hereditary rulership by saying that "in its original principles," every government was an "equal republic." He had
broached the idea on which Paine's criticism of the English
constitution was based—that a "simple" thing is better than
a "complex" thing. Paine's and Priestley's agreement on this
point is arresting, because this was a most unusual idea at
that time. In the eighteenth century, people were accustomed
to conceiving life in terms of an artificial mechanism; thus the
more complicated machine appeared as the more nearly
perfect one; and, consequently, intricate mechanical con-

cepts such as "balance of power" and "mixed government" were favorite principles of political thought. Yet the greatest similarity between Paine and Priestley is to be found in their descriptions of the emergence of representative government as a necessary result of a gradual increase in population. Paine's passages on this topic seem a paraphrase of Priestley's words; if one reads the respective sections of the two books, one will be inclined to assume that Paine wrote *Common Sense* with Priestley's pamphlet on his desk.

The group of utilitarian philosophers to which Priestley belonged had very definite ideas on foreign affairs; they were pacifists and, therefore, bitter enemies of England's involvement in Continental quarrels. Paine followed the same pattern of thought.

Since the main purpose of Paine's pamphlet was to point out the advantages of an immediate declaration of independence, it was from this angle that he viewed the question of foreign affairs. He held the opinion that a declaration of independence would procure the immediate assistance of France and Spain. As long as the bonds between England and the colonies were not formally severed, France and Spain would never dare to help the colonies; they would fear a possible betrayal by a compromise between England and the colonies, not to mention that their help would be a striking violation of international law. Paine claimed, moreover, that independence would have advantages lasting far beyond the present emergency. It would secure peace for America: "France and Spain never were, nor perhaps ever will be, our enemies as Americans, but as our being subjects of Great Britain." There is not "a single advantage that this continent can reap by being connected with Great Britain." On the contrary, America's "plan is commerce, and that, well attended to, will secure us the peace and friendship of all Europe; because it is the interest of all Europe to have America a free port." These arguments were summarized in the famous sentence: "Any submission to, or dependence on, Great Britain, tends directly to involve this continent in European wars and quarrels . . . . As Europe is our market for trade, we ought to form no partial connection with any part of it. It is the true interest of America to steer clear of European contentions."

Thus Paine had a definite program for American foreign policy. He advocated not only separation from England but also renunciation of all political alliances; America should become a free port to serve the commercial interests of all nations. The two arguments on which this program was based were America's peculiar geographical position and her trading interests, both of which would protect her from attacks, because all states were interested in maintaining trade with America. There is a striking similarity between this program and the ideas of the English radicals who had attacked England's "Continental connections" and had emphasized the peculiarity of the English geographical situation and her special interests as a trading nation. Paine himself mentioned in *Common Sense* the "miseries of Hanover's last war," thereby showing that the English parallel was uppermost in his mind. In his program on foreign policy, Paine applied to America the ideas and concepts of the English controversy on the merits of "Continental connections."

With the appearance of *Common Sense,* a change took place in the American political scene. Uncertainty and hesitation were overcome; the movement toward independence became an irresistible force. This is well known. But it deserves to be mentioned that by giving precise formulation to what were felt to be the needs of America, *Common Sense* also laid out the course which the new republic would follow in its foreign policy. For a long time, every utterance on foreign policy starts from Paine's words and echoes his thoughts.

CHAPTER III

Novus Ordo Seculorum:

ENLIGHTENMENT IDEAS ON DIPLOMACY

I

PAINE's *Common Sense* was published in January 1776. Throughout the following months, the movement for independence gained increasing momentum. The final stage in the chain of events which led to the foundation of an independent United States was reached on June 7, 1776, when the Congress entered upon the consideration of R. H. Lee's resolution "that these United Colonies are, and of right ought to be, free and independent States, that they are absolved from all allegiance to the British crown, and that all political connection between them and the State of Great Britain is, and ought to be, totally dissolved; that it is expedient forthwith to take the most effectual measures for forming foreign Alliances; that a plan of confederation be prepared and transmitted to the respective Colonies for their consideration and approbation."[1]

Confederation, foreign alliances, and independence were presented as interconnected measures in this motion; its pivot was the urgent need for foreign assistance. Because of the difficult economic situation which had developed in the colonies, Congress had been forced to admit the failure of a policy, the main weapon of which had been the stoppage

[1] *Journals of the Continental Congress*, ed. Worthington Chauncey Ford, vol. v, Washington 1906, p. 425.

of trade between the colonies and the outside world. Thus on April 6, 1776, the Congress ordered the opening of American ports to the ships of all nations except Great Britain. Because of the British supremacy on the seas and the lack of an American navy, the success of this measure depended on the willingness of foreign powers not only to receive American trade, but also to protect it. The American leaders were aware, however, that no foreign power could dare to take the risky step of assisting the American rebels without having a definite guarantee that some stable regime would be created on the North American continent and that return to British rule would be made impossible. "Confederation" and "independence" were the necessary prerequisites for securing "foreign alliances."

But what did the Americans understand by "foreign alliances"? When John Adams, a few years later, reviewed the events of the summer of 1776, he declared that in the debates of 1776, on the application to foreign powers he had laid it down as a first principle that "we should calculate all our measures and foreign negotiations in such a manner, as to avoid a too great dependence upon any one power of Europe—to avoid all obligations and temptations to take any part in future European wars; that the business of America with Europe was commerce, not politics or war."[2] Yet in 1776, Adams had been a zealous supporter of Lee's resolution which had recommended the conclusion of foreign alliances. At present, the term "alliance" is understood to mean the establishment of cooperation in the political sphere among the contracting parties. If John Adams saw no contradiction between a support of Lee's resolution and an avoidance of political obligations, he must have used the

[2] John Adams to Secretary Livingston, February 5, 1783, printed in John Adams, *Works*, ed. Charles Francis Adams, vol. VIII, Boston 1853, p. 35.

word "alliance" in a sense different from the present-day meaning of a close political bond.

It can probably be said that our identification of "alliance" with political or even political-military commitments derives from the fact that in the modern world, diplomatic instruments which contain political or political-military arrangements are sharply separated from those concerned with regulations of trade, tariffs, and navigation. Yet this separation of political treaties from commercial treaties began only in the eighteenth century. In the Peace of Utrecht of 1713 ending the hostilities of the War of the Spanish Succession between England and France, political and commercial arrangements were dealt with for the first time in separate documents. This new pattern was only slowly adopted; throughout the eighteenth century, one and the same treaty could still contain arrangements about political, commercial, and economic questions. Thus there are many nuances in the seventeenth and eighteenth centuries between the opposite types of the "traité d'alliance offensive et défensive," clearly designating a political-military bond, and the "traité de commerce," exclusively concerned with trade. Such names as "traité d'alliance et de commerce," "traité de paix, de navigation, et de commerce," "traité de navigation et commerce," "traité de marine," suggest the variety of content which could be contained in a single diplomatic document. In the terminology of the eighteenth century, all such treaties established "alliances."

Thus Adams' view that one could have alliances with foreign powers without making political commitments finds its explanation in the usage of the eighteenth century; other Americans used the term "alliance" in the same loose way. In the first six months of the year 1776, before Lee's resolution made the question of foreign alliances an issue of practical politics, the problem had been frequently discussed;

and the ambiguity of the term "alliance" had resulted in a great variety of contradictory opinions about the consequences of concluding foreign alliances. They were looked upon with fear, but they were also regarded as the instrument by which America could obtain the necessary assistance without restrictions on her freedom of action. One of the reasons given against the conclusion of alliances with foreign powers was that the bond which had existed between England and the colonies in the past had been an "alliance";[3] Britain had provided military protection for the granting of commercial advantages on the part of the colonies. An alliance with a foreign power might lead to the same consequences which the "alliance" with Britain had had; "an expedient of this kind" would lead the colonists into "having their allies, at last, for their masters."[4] It would produce the exchange of domination by one power for domination by another. To avoid this danger, it was suggested that the alliance be restricted to "external assistance";[5] a distinction was to be made between cooperation on land and cooperation at sea. While the French navy should be allowed to play a part in the war, no assistance by a French army should be accepted. In general, Americans were very optimistic about the prospects of receiving the protection of the French navy for American trade without having to make political commitments in return; most Americans believed that the separation of the American colonies from Britain's

[3] For instance, Thomas Paine, *Complete Writings*, ed. Philip S. Foner, vol. I, New York 1945, p. 20; John Adams, *Works*, vol. IV, pp. 110, 114; *Letters of Members of the Continental Congress*, ed. Edmund C. Burnett, VOL. I, Washington 1921, p. 369; *American Archives*, ed. Peter Force, fourth series, vol. V, Washington 1844, p. 1208; and, most of all, Franklin's "Vindication" of 1775, see Benjamin Franklin, *Works*, ed. Jared Sparks, vol. V, Philadelphia 1840, pp. 83-90.

[4] Cato's "Fifth Letter to the People of Pennsylvania," *American Archives*, fourth series, vol. V, pp. 542-543.

[5] Richard Henry Lee to Landon Carter, June 2, 1776, *Letters of Members of the Continental Congress*, vol. I, p. 469.

imperial system and the possibility of trade with the colonies would be regarded by the French as a sufficient attraction. Other Americans were less sanguine. When Franklin wrote about the possibility of exchanging "commerce for friend-ship,"[6] he seems to have felt that a somewhat more substan-tial inducement in the form of some monopoly, at least for a definite period, must be offered to France. Thus when the contingency of entering into alliances with foreign powers was debated in the early part of 1776, such a measure com-prised a wide range of possibilities: a purely commercial treaty, or a treaty with commercial obligations from the American side and political-military obligations from the French side, or a treaty with reciprocal political commit-ments. When Lee proposed his resolution on June 7, 1776, the thinking in the colonies had not yet crystallized into a clear conception of the kind of "alliance" America should conclude. Only when the Congress began to deliberate on the treaty to be proposed to France and on the instruction to be given to the American negotiators did the ideas on this problem take a definite form, a form which was striking and novel.

The external story of the further events is clearly estab-lished. On June 11, 1776, in consequence of Lee's resolution, a committee was appointed to prepare the model of a treaty to be proposed to the French court. This committee handed in its report on July 18 and the report was discussed in the Continental Congress on August 22, 27, and 29. Then the Congress referred the report back to the committee for amendment and for preparation of instructions to be given to the American agents. On September 17, this final report of the committee was made to the Congress, and the latter's agreement to the prepared instructions was given on September 24. Two days later, Benjamin Franklin, Silas

---

[6] Franklin to Joseph Priestley, July 7, 1775, *ibid.*, p. 156.

Deane, and Thomas Jefferson were appointed commissioners to France.

The internal story behind these factual events is much more difficult to disentangle. For its reconstruction we have only a few documents—the Model Treaty and the instructions—and brief remarks in the letters and memoirs of the main actors.

John Adams was a member of the committee entrusted with the preparation of the Model Treaty, and he was assigned to draft this document. Adams must be considered as the chief architect of the Model Treaty and its accompanying instructions. He had given much thought to the subject before he entered upon this task. In March 1776, evidently influenced by Paine's *Common Sense,* he had set down on paper his ideas as to the "connection we may safely form" with France and arrived at the following formula: "1. No political connection. Submit to none of her authority, receive no governors or officers from her. 2. No military connection. Receive no troops from her. 3. Only a commercial connection; that is, make a treaty to receive her ships into our ports; let her engage to receive our ships into her ports; furnish us with arms, cannon, saltpetre, powder, duck, steel."[7] How fundamental these ideas were for him can be deduced from the fact that they also appear in letters which he wrote in the spring of 1776. He urged the necessity of sending ambassadors to foreign courts "to form with them, at least with some of them, commercial treaties of friendship and alliance";[8] and when the dangers to American freedom of an alliance with a foreign power were pointed out to him, he stressed that in recommending foreign alliances, he was thinking only of a contractual safeguard of America's trade

[7] John Adams, *Works,* vol. II, pp. 488-489.
[8] John Adams to William Cushing, June 9, 1776, *Letters of Members of the Continental Congress,* vol. I, p. 478.

relations. "I am not for soliciting any political connection, or military assistance, or indeed naval, from France. I wish for nothing but commerce, a mere marine treaty with them."[9]

The Model Treaty was intended to realize the ideas which John Adams had previously developed—namely, that alliance did not imply a political bond and that America's contacts with outside powers should be limited to trade relations. When Adams began to draft the Model Treaty, Franklin put into his hand "a printed volume of treaties" in which he had made some pencil marks beside certain articles. Adams found "some of these judiciously selected, and I took them, with others which I found necessary, into the draught."[10] A comparison of the Model Treaty with earlier documents reveals that Adams relied heavily on two particular treaties: the treaty between James II and Louis XIV of November 16, 1686, concerning the neutrality of the American colonies in case of a conflict between England and France; and the commercial treaty between England and France of 1713. Most of the stipulations of the Model Treaty concerned with the regulation of trade, navigation, and fishing—which is to say, the greater part of the Model Treaty—are taken from these treaties. In other words, agreements which regulated the commercial relations between England and France were used as patterns for the Model Treaty, and, in that, the United States took the place of England. It seems likely that Adams chose the commercial treaty between England and France of 1713 also because its regulations had been of a most liberal character. The liberal spirit which inspired the American draft is reflected particularly in the articles dealing with trade in wartime. The Model Treaty contained a precisely circumscribed and extremely limited list of contraband goods: even foodstuffs

[9] John Adams to John Winthrop, June 23, 1776, *ibid.*, p. 502.
[10] John Adams, *Works*, vol. II, p. 516.

and naval stores were excluded from it. Furthermore, neutrals should have the right to trade with belligerents, and the principle was laid down that free ships make free goods. The strongest indication of this tendency towards complete freedom in trade can be found, however, in the first two articles of the Model Treaty, which were concerned with the establishment of basic principles for the future commercial relations between France and America. These articles go beyond anything that Adams could have taken from the treaties between England and France. The Model Treaty suggested that the French should treat the inhabitants of the United States with regard to duties and imports as natives of France and vice versa; moreover, they "shall enjoy all other the Rights, Liberties, Priviledges, Immunities and Exemptions in Trade, Navigation and Commerce, in passing from one port [Part] thereof to another, and in going to and from the same, from and to any Part of the World, which the said Natives, or Companies enjoy."[11] The "instructions" added that only if "his most Christian Majesty shall not consent" to these articles, the commissioners should try to get the French agreement to a most-favored-nation clause.[12] The latter was proposed only as a less attractive alternative if a reciprocity clause could not be obtained. The fundamental concepts behind these proposals are evident and, as far as the practical policy of the period is concerned, striking: in drafting the Model Treaty, the colonists were thinking not only of France but also of other powers. They were, in effect, creating a general pattern for future commercial treaties. Whereas usually commercial conventions were sources of friction and instruments of power politics reinforcing political alliances by commercial preferences, the Americans wanted to establish a commercial system of free-

---

[11] *Journals of the Continental Congress*, vol. v, p. 769.
[12] *Ibid.*, p. 813.

dom and equality which would eliminate all cause for tension and political conflicts.

Although John Adams might have wanted to limit the Model Treaty to questions of trade and navigation, a number of political questions had to be taken up. Thus French protection was to replace the former English protection of American ships against the attacks of the Barbary States. Moreover, a number of articles were concerned with the problems which had arisen from the war against the British and had forced the colonists into "their application to foreign powers." It was stipulated that American ships should be protected and convoyed by their allies and that France should give up any claim to territories of the North American continent, while the Americans would not oppose a French conquest of the West Indies.

Since both countries—France and the United States— were moving in a sharply anti-English direction, would it not be desirable that they agree on common action for war and peace and that the conditions of their political cooperation be clearly defined? A treaty with the colonial rebels would unavoidably involve France in a war with England; and for most of the colonial leaders, this was the purpose of an agreement with France. Hence some statement about the reciprocal obligations of the two powers fighting against the same potential enemy was necessary. The manner in which the Model Treaty dealt with this question was surprising, as it revealed the Americans' disinclination to be forced into a political bond with an outside power even under pressure of war. Article 8 stated that in case the alliance with the United States should involve France in war with England, the United States would not assist England in such a war. The promise offered in this article—namely, that America would not use the opportunity of an Anglo-French war for coming to an understanding with England—was little more than a matter of course. What is astounding is how little the Americans were willing to offer. Political and military cooperation with France was to be avoided even if France should enter the war against England.

In the instructions for the American negotiators, it was said that this "article will probably be attended with some Difficulty,"[13] and the article was explained by an unusually long comment. Clearly the article had evoked a heated debate in the committee. A number of members felt that such love of principle defeated its own purpose and that a somewhat more realistic approach was necessary to obtain French participation in the war. Thus they wanted to include in the instructions a paragraph which would have given the American negotiators permission to offer a greater inducement to France: reconquest of the islands in the West Indies which France had ceded to England after the Seven Years' War: "If the Court of France cannot be prevailed on to engage in the War with Great Britain for any consideration already proposed in this Treaty, you are hereby authorized to agree as a further inducement, that these United States will wage the war in union with France, not make peace with Great Britain until the latter France shall gain the possession of those Islands in the West Indies formerly called Nieutral, and which by the Treaty of Paris were ceded to G. Britain: provided France shall make the conquest of these Islands an early object of the War and prosecute the same with sufficient force."[14] However, the majority of Congress was not willing to make commitments about territorial changes, and this paragraph was omitted from the final instructions. Some concessions were made to those who cared more about getting France into the war than about principles of foreign policy. The commissioners were entitled to make some additional offers: the United States was willing to

[13] *Ibid.*, pp. 814-815.   [14] *Ibid.*, p. 817.

guarantee that it would grant to no other power trading privileges which it had not granted to the French king; furthermore, in case France should become involved in the present war, neither France nor the United States would conclude peace without notifying the other power six months ahead.

The striking thing about the Model Treaty and the accompanying instructions is that, although the Americans were in a desperate situation in which they looked anxiously for foreign help, their leaders insisted on proposals which were entirely alien to the spirit of the diplomatic practice of the time.

II

It was a long journey from the simple brick building of the State House in Philadelphia, with its unpretentious wood paneling, to the palaces of Paris and Versailles, abounding in marble and rosewood, chinoiseries, mirrors, and silk. How did the American leaders have the courage to proffer to the French government, ensconced in eighteenth-century splendor, a treaty which challenged all the diplomatic traditions of which France was the foremost practitioner?

The Americans were convinced of the immense value of the offer which they made to France: the ending of the English monopoly of trade with North America. The consequence would be not only to increase French economic prosperity, but also to weaken England, France's old rival. The Americans may have somewhat overestimated the extent to which the opening of the American ports to the ships of all nations would revolutionize the European state system. But in the American view, France would gain such far-reaching advantages that America had a right to determine the nature of the relationship which, in the future, should exist between America and the European powers.

The Model Treaty with which the Americans formulated their concept of this relationship shows the impact of the program which Paine had set forth in *Common Sense*. The Model Treaty and the accompanying instructions were designed to keep America out of European struggles and to secure for her peace and freedom by making all European powers interested partners in American trade. But behind these documents there lay an attitude which leads beyond the image which Paine had given of America's role in foreign policy. Paine's ideas are products of the age in which he was born, of the Enlightenment; but in *Common Sense*, he did not share its optimism. To Paine, the world, with the exception of America, was rotten and lost. "Freedom hath been hunted around the globe. Asia and Africa have long expelled her, Europe regards her like a stranger, and England hath given her warning to depart." America was to be preserved as the last bulwark of liberty, "an asylum for mankind." This censure of Europe corresponded to feelings deeply rooted in America's colonial past and facilitated the acceptance of the ideas of *Common Sense* in America. But American intellectual life was also strongly imbued with the spirit of the Enlightenment. Although most Americans may have agreed with Paine's condemnation of Europe's political and social life as it existed at the time, not all of them shared Paine's gloomy prognostications for Europe's future; many were in accord with the Enlightenment belief in progress and were convinced that a new and better age in the history of the human race was approaching. They believed the American Revolution had started a great experiment; they felt they were setting a pattern which the rest of the world would follow. Thus the Model Treaty had a double face. It was intended, on the one hand, as an instrument to achieve an independent existence for America, secure from the corrupting influence of Europe. On the other hand, by eliminating purely political issues like territorial settlements, by focussing on the regulation of commercial relations, and by placing them on such a liberal basis that the arrangements between France and America could easily be extended to the nations of the whole world, the Americans transformed the Model Treaty into a pattern for all future diplomatic treaties. The Americans entered the European scene as the representatives of the diplomacy of a new era. They did not feel confronted by an entirely hostile world. They might find little sympathy for their ideas with the rulers of France, who thought in terms of traditional diplomacy. But they felt they had many friends: their allies were all the progressive minds of Europe, the writers and thinkers whom we now call "the philosophes."

The philosophes' ideas on foreign policy and diplomacy throw light on the broad background from which the American views on this topic developed. The philosophes confirmed the Americans in their outlook on diplomacy and, for a number of years, were an important factor in determining the course of American foreign policy; finally, they infused a lasting idealistic element into the American attitude toward foreign affairs.

The views of the philosophes both on foreign policy and on domestic policy were based on the conviction that history had reached the end of a long and tortuous development; the contrasts and conflicts of the past would now be resolved in a great synthesis, and a permanent order could be accomplished. The confidence of the philosophes in the near approach of a golden age had its foundation in a peculiar constellation of historical factors.

We have spoken of the change in the political system of Europe signified by the Peace of Utrecht. One of the aspects of this change was the growing awareness of the importance of the non-European parts of the globe. The stipulations of the Treaty of Utrecht covered the entire world and thereby demonstrated to what extent the great European powers, though they remained of central importance, drew their strength from the resources of other continents. This is reflected in Turgot's statement that the trend of the time was to make the boundaries of the political world "become identical with those of the physical world."[15]

This feeling that one civilization now encompassed the whole world was reinforced by the astounding growth of economic interdependence. In the centers of European civilization, people could rely on having a regular supply of goods from all over the world: sugar from the West Indies, tea and china from the Far East, coffee and chocolate from the Americas and Africa. The barriers that existed seemed artificial and ephemeral in comparison with the fine net by which the merchants tied the individuals of the different nations together like "threads of silk."[16] As Sédaine says in his famous comedy *Le philosophe sans le savoir*, the merchants—whether they are English, Dutch, Russian, or Chinese—do not serve a single nation; they serve everyone and are citizens of the whole world. Commerce was believed to bind the nations together and to create not only a community of interests but also a distribution of labor among them—a new comprehensive principle placing the isolated sovereign nations in a higher political unit. In the eighteenth century, writers were likely to say that the various nations belonged to "one society"; it was stated that all states together formed "a family of nations," and the whole globe a "general and unbreakable confederation."[17]

[15] Turgot, *Oeuvres*, ed. Gustave Schelle, vol. I, Paris 1913, p. 263.
[16] Michel-Jean Sédaine, *Le philosophe sans le savoir*, act II, scene 4.
[17] For instance, Mercier de la Rivière, "L'ordre naturel et essentiel des Sociétés Politiques, 1767," in *Collection des Économistes et des Reformateurs Sociaux de la France*, ed. Edgar Depitre, Paris 1910, pp. 242-252; Le Trosne, *De l'Ordre Social*, Paris 1777, pp. 355,

The social force which carried this development was the bourgeoisie. In the eighteenth century, its members became conscious of being a main prop of social life; they felt entitled to have all obstacles to the development of their interests eliminated. The philosophes gave the claims of this class an ideological form. They did for the bourgeoisie what intellectuals usually do when a new and rising class wants to break the restraints which keep it in a subordinate position. Then intellectuals identify the cause of a class with the cause of the human race in general and explain that the fight is a fight for freedom against tyranny, rather than for special interests against privileges and suppression by a ruling group. The triumph of the new class is to be a victory of humanity, the final solution of all historical conflicts.

Most of the eighteenth-century philosophes were French. France was the most powerful nation of Europe, the theater in which the issues of the century were fought out. In the economically less advanced countries of Central and Eastern Europe, the power of the feudal and agrarian ruling group could not yet be seriously challenged. In England, as a result of the civil wars and revolutions of the previous century, the commercial classes had gained a steadily increasing influence and were becoming gradually amalgamated with the ruling group. In France, monarchy and nobility were still in exclusive political control, but the bourgeoisie had become a powerful economic and social factor; the forces of the old order and of the new faced each other in almost equal poise. Moreover, although the wars of Louis XIV had brought France to the zenith of power in Europe, they had eventually threatened to carry

392-393; Gaillard, "Les Avantages de La Paix, 1767," in Gabriel-Henri Gaillard, *Mélanges Académiques, Poétiques, Littéraires, Philologiques*, vol. i, Paris 1806, p. 66.

her beyond that point. The French people had entered the
century exhausted and dispirited. The traditional policy of
territorial expansion on the Continent and the drive for
European hegemony had lost much of its glamour. Thus the
great concern of the philosophes was domestic policy.

If the ideas of the philosophes on foreign policy have been
studied less than those on domestic policy, this one-sided-
ness of modern interests corresponds to the order of value
which the philosophes themselves assigned to these two fields
of political activity. Their thesis was that the great role which
foreign affairs played in the political life of their time was
one of the most fundamental evils of the existing political
system. D'Argenson has most succinctly formulated this basic
attitude of the philosophes with regard to the relationship
between domestic and foreign affairs. "The true purpose of
the science called politics is to perfect the interior of a state
as much as possible. Flatterers assure the princes that the
interior is there only to serve foreign policy. Duty tells them
the opposite."[18]

The philosophes directed a systematic attack against the
view which regarded foreign policy as the center and culmination of political activities. They assailed the entire concept of man which complements this philosophy of power
politics that stresses the qualities of physical prowess, honor,
and obedience. The high evaluation of military virtues is a
"dangerous prejudice, a carry-over from barbarism, a rem-
nant of the former chaos."[19] "True fame consists not in the
glory which the stupidity of the people connects with conquests and which the still more stupid historians love to

[18] D'Argenson, *Considérations sur le Gouvernement Ancient et
Présent de la France*, Amsterdam 1764, p. 18.
[19] *Ibid.*, p. 20.

praise to the point of boring the reader";[20] if the right name were to be given to conquests "which for so long have been praised as heroism,"[21] they would be called crimes.

The existing methods of diplomacy were so much geared towards power politics and war that they could never serve the opposite purpose—the preservation of peace. The main target of the philosophes was the assumption that the only possibility and guarantee for peace lay in the maintenance of a balance of power among the states. There is hardly a philosophe and reformer who does not inveigh against the idea of balance of power, "this favorite idea of newspapers and coffee-house politicians."[22] This idea, "reducing the whole science of politics to knowledge of a single word, pleases both the ignorance and the laziness of the ministers, of ambassadors and their clerks."[23] In contrast to the ostensible aim of promoting peace, balance of power had, it was said, always done harm to a system of lasting peace and was opposed to it. The reason was that "the system of balance of power is a system of resistance, consequently of disturbance, of shocks and of explosions."[24] With the overthrow of this central concept of eighteenth-century diplomacy, the other concerns of the traditional diplomacy were also reevaluated and shown up in their futility and dangerousness. According to the philosophes, the conclusion of treaties and alliances, the most significant activity of eighteenth-century diplomacy, would not serve to establish friendly relations among states; treaties are nothing but "temporary armi-

[20] Condillac, "Le Commerce et le Gouvernement, 1776," in Condillac, *Oeuvres Complètes*, vol. IV, Paris 1821, p. 278.

[21] Condorcet, "Discours de Réception à l'Académie Française," in Condorcet, *Oeuvres*, ed. A. C. O'Connor and M. F. Arago, vol. I, Paris 1847-1849, p. 396.

[22] [Mirabeau], *L'Ami des Hommes ou Traité de la Population*, nouvelle édition 1759, 3rd part, p. 368.

[23] Mably, *"Principes des Négociations,"* in Abbé de Mably, *Collection Complète des Oeuvres*, vol. V, Paris 1784, p. 66.

[24] Gaillard, *loc.cit.*, pp. 79-80.

stices"[25] and alliances "preparations for treason."[26] Even when they are called defensive alliances, they are "in reality always of an offensive nature."[27] Diplomatic activity, thus being identical with double-dealing and pursuing purposes different from those it openly avows, needs to wrap itself in secrecy and has become an "obscure art which hides itself in the folds of deceit, which fears to let itself be seen and believes it can succeed only in the darkness of mystery."[28] Secrecy, therefore, is not—as the diplomats pretend—necessary for the efficient fulfillment of their functions; it only proves that they are conspirators planning crimes. Diderot, in a satirical piece entitled "Political Principles of Rulers," has summarized the views of the philosophes on the diplomacy of their time. "Make alliances only in order to sow hatred. . . . Incite wars among my neighbors and try to keep it going. . . . Have no ambassadors in other countries, but spies. . . . To be neutral means to profit from the difficulties of others in order to improve one's own situation."[29] Though different writers made different aspects of diplomacy—secrecy or formality of etiquette—the chief butts of their criticism, they were all in agreement that diplomacy could not be reformed by redressing any single abuse. The evil inherent in diplomacy could be removed only by a complete change in the attitude of those who ruled. Foreign affairs showed most clearly the ills of a world not yet ruled by reason. "The blind passions of the princes"[30] were the cause of wars, conquests, and all the

[25] Rousseau, "Extrait du Projet de Paix Perpétuelle de M. L'Abbé de Saint Pierre," in J. J. Rousseau, *Political Writings*, ed. C. E. Vaughan, vol. i, Cambridge 1915, p. 369.

[26] Guillaume-Thomas Raynal, *Histoire Philosophique et Politique des Établissements et du Commerce des Européens dans les deux Indes*, vol. vi, Geneve 1781, p. 284.

[27] D'Argenson, *op.cit.*, p. 327.

[28] Le Trosne, *op.cit.*, p. 395.

[29] Diderot, "Principes de Politique des Souverains," in Diderot, *Oeuvres Complètes*, ed. J. Assézat, vol. ii, Paris 1875, pp. 461-502.

[30] Diderot in article "Paix" in *Dictionnaire Encyclopédique*, in Diderot, *Oeuvres Complètes*, vol. xvi, p. 188.

miseries accompanying them. A favorite story of the eighteenth century illustrating the arbitrariness which dominated foreign policy was the story of the palace window: Louvois, fearing disgrace because Louis XIV had expressed displeasure with Louvois' arrangements concerning the construction of the windows of the Trianon, instigated the King to renew the war against the Hapsburgs in order to divert his attention from architectural matters. As long as foreign policy continued to be determined by passions, by whims and arbitrary proclivities, diplomacy could be nothing else but "the art of intrigue."[31]

If one wants to reduce this whole complex of eighteenth-century ideas on diplomacy to a simple formula, it can be summarized as the establishment of a rule of reason. It is the same solution which the philosophes had for the problems of domestic policy. In view of the pre-eminence which they gave domestic over foreign affairs, they considered the introduction of a new and peaceful era in foreign policy dependent on a reorganization of domestic policy. It would even be enough to put the policy of France on a new basis. Since France was the hub in the wheel of European politics, the other nations would quickly follow the French lead; a new period in world history would begin.

Yet how could this change be effected? As much as the eighteenth-century reformers agreed on the basic concepts which we have sketched above, they differed on how their ideas could be realized. Some looked for a solution along conservative, others along radical, democratic lines.

Among those who had a more conservative outlook were the physiocrats. A great number of the philosophes—some in a more, others in a less orthodox way—belonged to the physiocratic school. Although today physiocracy is usually regarded as having propounded an original and important

[31] Mably, *Oeuvres*, vol. v, p. 17.

economic doctrine, the significance of physiocratic theories in the eighteenth century seemed to reach far beyond the economic sphere and to range over the entire structure of social and political life. The physiocrats called their political theory "economic policy," not because they were concerned solely with economic questions, but because, to them, economics and politics were identical. They believed that all political problems would be solved if the right economic principles were followed and the right economic measures adopted. The contrast to "economic policy" was the "old policy," the "false policy," or "power politics"; all of these terms were alternately used. "The essence of power politics consists of divergence of interests, that of economic policy of unity of interests—the one leads to war, frustrations, destruction, the other to social integration, co-operation, and free and peaceful sharing of the fruits of work."[32] The physiocrats elaborated this contrast between "the old policy" and "the economic policy," between an "artificial" and a "natural" political situation, with great gusto and especially emphasized that, as a result of the artificiality of the "old policy," dealings had to be shrouded in secrecy and mystery. The diplomats had to be actors—"competitors in grimaces"[33]— and each nation was barricaded behind its own frontiers, intent on making commercial treaties to its own advantage and to the disadvantage of its neighbor. In contrast, the new world in which the "economic policy" was to be realized would have an unrestricted exchange of goods. From mutual interdependence would emerge the realization that increase in one nation's wealth means increased wealth for all other nations, and that the interests of all nations are identical; consequently, there would be no advantage in enlarging one's

[32] Baudeau, "Première Introduction à la Philosophie Économique, 1767," in *Physiocrates*, ed. Eugène Daire, vol. ii, Paris 1846, p. 742.
[33] [Mirabeau], *op.cit.*, p. 26.

own territory and combatting one's neighbor. A single measure, namely, the establishment of free trade, would bring about this miraculous change; it was up to the rulers of the states to take this one decisive measure. The physiocrats were favorites of many princes, and their faith in the power of reason was so strong that they believed in the probability of persuading the rulers of the states to make this change. They were no opponents of despotism; on the contrary, they were confident that the new order could be introduced quite easily with and by means of the prince's absolute power.

Other philosophes believed that the physiocrats were deceiving themselves by trusting in princely absolutism. These more radical thinkers saw despotism as an integral part of the old order which had to be overcome. The decisive step in establishing the new order was a change in political leadership; the people themselves had to take over control of political life. These writers were concerned with the problem of how to achieve an effective popular control of foreign policy. Condorcet, who was particularly interested in this question, constructed a mechanism which he considered suitable for this purpose. No convention between nations should be valid without approval of the legislative body. Moreover, as a further safeguard, he demanded that political treaties should be ratified by the single districts of a state. In case of an enemy attack, war might be declared, but only by the legislative; and a declaration of war would have to be followed immediately by new elections, which would give the people the opportunity to express their views on the war. Evidently Condorcet had no doubt that the people would always be peace-loving; the practical issue was to remove all obstacles to a direct expression of the popular will. Condorcet regarded diplomats as such an obstacle, as unnecessary middlemen. He had no use for them, nor for diplomatic arrangements establishing automatic obligations by which the freedom of action of a nation would be bound. "Alliance treaties seem to me so dangerous and so little useful that I think it is better to abolish them entirely in time of peace. They are only means by which the rulers of states precipitate the people into wars from which they benefit either by covering up their mistakes or by carrying out their plots against freedom, and for which the emergency serves as a pretext."[34] The picture which the philosophes envisaged of the relations among nations after the rule of reason had been established was implied in their criticism of the existing foreign policy: the former would be the reverse of the latter. Foreign policy should follow moral laws. There should be no difference between the "moral principles" which rule the relations among individuals and "moral principles" which rule the relations among states. Diplomacy should be "frank and open."[35] Formal treaties would be unnecessary; political alliances should be avoided particularly. Commercial conventions should refrain from all detailed regulations establishing individual advantages and privileges; they should limit themselves to general arrangements stating the fundamental rules and customs of trade and navigation. In such a world, the connection among the different states would rest in the hands not of governments but of individuals trading with each other.

If this picture of the foreign policy of the future was not very precise, there was a special reason. Foreign policy and diplomacy were regarded as typical phenomena of the *ancien régime;* they owed their importance to the fact that the rulers followed false ideals and egoistic passions instead of reason. The logical consequence was that in a reformed world, based on reason, foreign policy and diplomacy would

[34] Condorcet, *Oeuvres*, vol. ix, p. 45; see also pp. 41-46.
[35] Le Trosne, *op.cit.*, p. 421.

become unnecessary, that the new world would be a world
without diplomats.

III

The visible symbol of the alliance between the new republic and the philosophes was the meeting of Franklin and
Voltaire in a Paris theater, embracing and kissing each other
while the public applauded. In our context, an equally significant encounter was that of John Adams with the Abbé de
Mably, a philosophe especially interested in the problems of
foreign affairs; according to Adams, Mably "spoke with great
indignation against the practice of lying, chicaning, and
finessing, in negotiations; frankness, candor, and probity,
were the only means of gaining confidence."[36]

The American commissioners were regarded in France as
representatives of a new diplomacy, and they behaved as
such. Silas Deane, whom the Continental Congress had dis-
patched to France even before independence had been declared, apologized in his first interview with the French
Foreign Minister, Count Vergennes, for any violation of
form which, inadvertently, he might have committed. "If
my commission or the mode of introducing the subject were
out of the usual course, I must rely on his goodness to make
allowances for a new-formed people, in circumstances al-
together unprecedented, and for their agent wholly un-
acquainted with Courts."[37] But Deane was not so humble as
he pretended to be to Vergennes. The same day, he wrote a
letter, full of contempt for ceremony and etiquette: "Parade
and Pomp have no charms in the eyes of a patriot, or even of
a man of common good sense."[38] When Franklin arrived to

[36] John Adams, *Works*, vol. III, p. 350.
[37] Silas Deane to the Secret Committee of Congress, August 18,
1776, in *New York Historical Society Collections*, vol. XIX: The Deane
Papers, vol. I, New York 1887, p. 201.
[38] *Ibid.*, p. 219.

negotiate the alliance with France, he emphasized by the simplicity of his dress—his shabby brown coat and unpowdered hair—that he was the representative of a new and uncorrupted world; Franklin was probably too much of a skeptic, even about his own enlightened beliefs, to be unaware of the propagandistic value of such an attention-provoking attire. Such subtle irony was entirely alien to John Adams, who followed the others to Europe. With deadly seriousness, Adams lectured Vergennes, who had advised him to make some adjustment to prevailing diplomatic customs, that "the dignity of North America does not consist in diplomatic ceremonials or any of the subtleties of etiquette; it consists solely in reason, justice, truth, the rights of mankind, and the interests of the nations of Europe."[39]

The diplomatic tasks with which the American agents had to deal could only strengthen their interest in the ideas of the philosophes on foreign policy. The initial concerns of the American diplomats were to conclude an alliance with France and to persuade other Continental powers to an attitude favorable to the American cause. Then they were occupied with the peace negotiations which extended over a long time. When peace with England had finally been concluded, the relations of the newly recognized republic to other powers had to be placed on a permanent footing. As varied as these changing tasks were, one issue was central in all of them: the replacement of the monopolistically arranged bonds between England and America by new regulations of trade and the settlement of the commercial relations which in the future should exist between America and the European powers.

As the Model Treaty, which Congress had adopted in 1776,

[39] John Adams to Vergennes, July 18, 1781, in *The Revolutionary Diplomatic Correspondence of the United States*, ed. Francis Wharton, vol. IV, Washington 1889, p. 590.

showed, the problems of trade had two aspects in the American mind: on the one hand, the Americans were anxious to avoid commercial treaties which would make American trade dependent on one power or a bloc of powers and, consequently, draw America into the political rivalries of the European powers. One aim of American policy, therefore, was to make trade as free as possible, because only a complete liberalization of trade could provide full security against the danger that close commercial relations might create a political dependency. On the other hand, the great importance of trade for American economic life made a smooth and uninterrupted flow of commerce urgently desirable; war, in which a strong seapower like England might stop ships and confiscate their goods as contraband or declare wide stretches of a coast as blockaded area into which no ships should sail, was the great threat, especially since America had no navy sufficient to protect her merchants. Another aim of American foreign policy, therefore, was to persuade other powers to the acceptance of principles of international law which would mitigate the impact of war on civilian life. America was particularly interested in having the neutral trade secured against interference so that "free ships would make free goods," in reducing the number of articles which could be confiscated as contraband, and in permitting application of the concept of blockade only to ports where the access could be effectively controlled.

Peace and commerce were also the focal ideas in the thinking of the philosophes on foreign policy. As we have seen, they were pacifists, deeply convinced of the uselessness of war and of the necessity to remove war from social life. They saw in commerce a great instrument for bringing about a new age of peace, if nations, instead of trying to further their own commerce at the expense of the commerce of another power, would permit a free flow of goods over the entire globe. Relations between nations would become purely commercial contacts, and the need for a political diplomacy with alliances and balance of power would disappear from the international scene. The ideas with which the Americans entered the political theater of Europe were facets of the larger complex of enlightened eighteenth-century thought.

The close connection between the ideas of the philosophes and American foreign policy appeared clearly in the negotiations about commercial treaties which developed after peace with England had been concluded. Even though Americans had tried to hold firm to the principles of the Model Treaty in the preceding years, their foreign policy had naturally been subordinated to the exigencies of the fight for survival and of gaining all possible support against Great Britain. But after the independence of the United States had been internationally recognized, a new and systematic attempt at realization of these principles could be made. Several powers had made feelers towards negotiations about commercial treaties with the United States. Congress was divided about the handling of this question. Some members felt that the main effort should be directed to the re-establishment of commercial relations with Britain; as one member wrote: "The Treaty with Britain presses upon us with much greater weight than with any other nation."[40] But the majority of Congress was not convinced that the gains which the re-establishment of trade with Britain might bring could compensate for the disadvantages involved in making special concessions to England and in abandoning the attempt to establish trade on an entirely general and liberal basis. The report which Congress finally accepted was drafted by Jef-

[40] Jefferson, *The Papers of Thomas Jefferson*, ed. Julian P. Boyd, vol. vii, Princeton 1953, p. 467.

ferson;[41] it maintained the principles which had first been stated in the Model Treaty of 1776. Great Britain was named as only one among many other states with which the conclusion of treaties of "amity and commerce" would be desirable. The idea of the report was "to form a general system of commerce by treaties with other nations," rejecting special preferences in favor of liberal rules applicable to all nations. Furthermore, the report suggested articles which might limit as far as possible disturbances of trade in wartime. It recommended the appointment of consuls and general consuls, but it stated that it was "inconvenient at present" "to keep ministers resident at the courts of Europe"; this last suggestion, however, was eliminated from the final version of the report. On the basis of this report, Congress issued instructions to its diplomatic agent on May 7, 1784.

The first negotiations to which these new instructions were applied were with Frederick the Great of Prussia. Negotiations with Denmark and Prussia had already been underway when Congress composed its new instructions. Jefferson, who had taken an active part in drafting them, was appointed to serve with Franklin and Adams as American negotiators in Europe. After Jefferson had arrived in Paris and had conferred with Franklin and Adams, he was charged with investigating the changes required to adjust the documents, which had been drafted in the previous negotiations in Europe, to the instructions which Congress had sent. Jefferson decided "to take up the subject as it were anew, to arrange the articles under classes, and while we are reforming the principles to reform also the language of treaties, which history alone and not grammar will justify. The articles may be rendered shorter and more conspicuous, by simplifying their stile and structure."[42] This intention

[41] *Ibid.*, vol. vi, pp. 393-400.
[42] *Ibid.*, vol. vii, pp. 476-477.

corresponded to a basic feature of Jefferson's mind; to him, style and structure were the external expression of clarity of thought. But one cannot help wondering whether, in simplifying the diplomatic language, Jefferson did not also intend to open the door for a diplomacy which would be divested of its character as a secret science.

Jefferson also drew up the communications which accompanied the revised treaty draft and which explained to the Prussian representative the reasons for the changes in the draft, particularly the insertion of two articles, one providing for the payment of war contraband in case of confiscation, the other protecting civilian life against the ravages of war. The American commissioners wrote that "it is for the interest of humanity in general, that the occasions of war, and the inducements to it should be diminished."[43] Measures to minimize the impact of war were a logical step in the continuing process of improving the law of nations. Since the beginnings of society when "war and extirpation was the punishment of injury," the development of the law of nations had gone forward "humanizing by degrees." Progress had been slow, so that "Ages have intervened between its several steps," but there was no reason why the law of nations should not "go on improving"; it was now a favorable occasion for accelerating this process: "As knowledge of late encreases rapidly, why should not those steps be quickened?" The enlightened belief in progress, coupled with the conviction of being at the threshold of a new age, found expression also in the further correspondence with the Prussian representative. The American commissioners felt that they were leading the way to an "object so valuable to mankind as the total emancipation of commerce and the bringing together all nations for a free intercommunication of happiness."[44] When finally the

[43] *Ibid.*, pp. 491, 492.
[44] *Ibid.*, vol. viii, p. 28.

treaty had been approved by Frederick the Great, John Adams expressed his enthusiasm in words which, although they might indicate some reservation about having these humane measures quickly adopted by the entire world, still suggest that Adams was satisfied with seeing the course of American foreign policy set towards utopia: "I am charmed to find the King do us the Honor to agree to the Platonic Philosophy of some of our Articles, which are at least a good Lesson to Mankind, and will derive more Influence from a Treaty ratified by the King of Prussia, than from the writings of Plato, or Sir Thomas More."[45]

The foreign policy of the young republic, with its emphasis on commerce and on avoidance of political connections, has usually been explained as a policy of isolation. Unquestionably, the English background of the ideas which served in the formation of the American outlook on foreign policy contained an isolationist element. However, if we place the ideas which guided early American foreign policy beside those of the European philosophes, it becomes clear that the isolationist interpretation is one-sided and incomplete: American foreign policy was idealistic and internationalist no less than isolationist.

In many minds, these two motives can be found interwoven in such a way that neither of the two elements can be regarded as predominant. This was characteristic of Jefferson. He remained opposed to diplomacy, which he considered as "the pest of the peace of the world, as the workshop in which nearly all the wars of Europe are manufactured."[46] In 1792, when a number of diplomatic nominations had been submitted to the Senate by Washington for approval, Jefferson suggested that diplomatic representatives should be sent by

[45] *Ibid.*, vol. vii, p. 465.
[46] Jefferson to William Short, January 23, 1804, "Documents," *American Historical Review*, vol. xxxiii (1927/8), p. 833.

America only to those countries where geographic closeness or interests of commerce demanded a permanent representation; this meant to London, Paris, Madrid, Lisbon, and The Hague. Also, these appointments should be kept "on the lowest grades admissible."[47] Later Jefferson wrote that "Consuls would do all the business we ought to have."[48] Jefferson's inclination towards the adoption of what he called an "a-diplomatic system" sprang from his fear that America might become involved in European politics but, at the same time, he wanted to set an example to the entire world. Jefferson was convinced that the relations between nations in the future would take forms different from those of the diplomacy of the past. His belief in the emergence of a new spirit in international relations is beautifully expressed in a letter to Madison of August 28, 1789. Jefferson pleaded for acknowledging the duties of gratitude in America's relations to France: the often heard view that power and force ruled in the relations between nations "were legitimate principles in the dark ages which intervened between antient and modern civilisation, but exploded and held in just horror in the 18th century. I know but one code of morality for man whether acting singly or collectively."[49]

Thus, although the American outlook on foreign affairs contained two different elements, they could be combined; and then they reinforced each other. But they could also be contradictory. Then those who were concerned with foreign policy suddenly swerved from one extreme to the other. Unexpected resistance or obstacles might turn the utopian hopes for an imminent "reformation, a kind of protestantism, in the

[47] Jefferson to a Committee of the Senate, January 4, 1792, in Thomas Jefferson, *Writings*, ed. Paul Leicester Ford, vol. i, New York 1892, p. 170.

[48] Jefferson to William Short, January 23, 1804, printed *loc.cit.*, p. 833.

[49] Jefferson to James Madison, August 28, 1789, in Jefferson, *Papers*, vol. xv, p. 367.

commercial system of the world"[50] into its reverse: demand for complete withdrawal from any contact with the outside world. The Americans might have to "recall their Ministers and send no more,"[51] as Adams wrote; or they ought "to stand to Europe precisely on the footing of China,"[52] as Jefferson formulated it. Yet it was immediately argued that this was not possible, because it would mean that the Americans would have to "give up the most of their commerce, and live by their agriculture."[53] It was "theory only."[54] In such moments, the egoistic insistence on isolation appeared no less unrealistic than the altruistic counsels of internationalism.

This dilemma was reflected in an episode which happened at the time of the end of the War of Independence. Indignation about the brutal way in which England used her seapower had led a number of European states to form a league of "armed neutrality," with the purpose of defending the right of neutrals on the sea. This policy not only corresponded to the general aims of the foreign policy of the United States but also raised the hope of gaining from these powers support in the struggle against Britain. Thus, the United States was anxious to join the league, but, because a belligerent power could hardly become a member of a league of neutrals, the American advances were rebuffed. When, with the signing of the preliminaries of peace, this obstacle was removed and the Netherlands urged America to participate actively in the policy of armed neutrality, Congress took another look at the possible practical consequences of such a policy; it was realized that the league would make the United

---

[50] John Adams, *Works*, vol. VIII, p. 298.

[51] John Adams to John Jay, February 26, 1783, *The Diplomatic Correspondence of the United States of America from 1783 to 1789*, vol. II, Washington 1837, p. 574.

[52] Jefferson, *Papers*, vol. VIII, p. 633.

[53] *The Diplomatic Correspondence of the United States from 1783 to 1789*, vol. II, p. 574.

[54] Jefferson, *Papers*, vol. VIII, p. 633.

States a member of a political bloc. Thus Congress, in a resolution[55] which admitted that "the liberal principles on which the said confederacy was established, are conceived to be in general favourable to the interests of nations, and particularly to those of the United States," rejected further negotiations about entry into the league, because "the true interest of these states requires that they should be as little as possible entangled in the politics and controversies of European nations." The principle of avoiding political connections proved to be incompatible with progress toward freeing commerce, which was the great hope for overcoming power politics.

But as contradictory as isolationism and internationalism could sometimes prove themselves to be, these contrasts could be overlooked; and they could be regarded as compatible with each other because there was a common factor between them, though only of a negative character: isolationism existed in a sphere of timelessness; internationalism existed in the future. Neither existed in the world of the present. Thus the attitudes which the young republic had adopted had not yet satisfactorily solved the problem—either practically or theoretically—of how to chart a course in the world as it was.

[55] *Journals of the Continental Congress*, vol. xxiv, p. 394.

CHAPTER IV

Ratio Status:

FOREIGN POLICY IN PRACTICE

I

WHEN, in 1791, Jean de Ternant, the first representative France sent to the United States after the Revolution of 1789, arrived in Philadelphia, he entered his mission with high hopes for close cooperation between the two nations. He confidently expected to find a government and people which shared the ideals and aspirations of the Revolution which was taking place in his country. But he was soon to discover that the spirit in which the American Republic had been founded was very different from that which inspired the French Revolution. A few months after his arrival he expressed contempt for the American republicans who cultivated "aristocratic distinctions" and treated with great earnestness "this ridiculous business of etiquette." Such emphasis on form and ceremony seemed to him "a puerility alien to the principles of our government and contrary to the customs of Europe."[1]

In retrospect this is an ironical situation. The same country whose agents had appeared in Paris in 1776 as protagonists of a new diplomatic style was reproached, fifteen years later, for its adherence to traditional and obsolete diplomatic punctilio.

Even if one deducts from Ternant's observation a certain

[1] Ternant to Montmorin, November 13, 1791, *American Historical Association, Annual Report, 1903*, vol. II, Washington 1904, p. 68.

amount of exaggeration evoked by annoyance over the cool-
ness of his reception in Philadelphia, the fact remains that a
great change had taken place in the American attitude toward ceremonies and etiquette. Closer acquaintance with
the European diplomatic scene had modified the views of
those who had come to France with proud feelings of superi-
ority over a world corrupted by a love for rank, distinctions,
and formalities. The American agents began to notice that
these arrangements, instead of being meaningless, reflected
the influence and the position which a country had in the
society of states. Soon after Deane's first interview with
Vergennes, in which the American had vaunted his ignorance
of diplomatic customs, Deane admitted that "something is
due to the dignity of old and powerful States or, if you
please, to their prejudices, in favor of long accustomed form
and etiquette."[2] It took John Adams longer to reach the same
conclusion, and at first he drew it very unwillingly. After an
audience with the British monarch he observed that "the essence of things are lost in ceremony in every country of
Europe," but he added: "We must submit to what we cannot
alter."[3] A few months later, Adams insisted on the necessity
of "splendor and magnificence" for a diplomat in Europe.
"To talk of republican simplicity is to make it worse."[4] Congress, on the other side of the ocean, had the same experience.
When the French envoy Gerard, the first official representative of a foreign power, arrived in Philadelphia, he was received with a ceremony which had been long and seriously
debated and worked out with a care which showed little of
the original scorn for etiquette.

[2] Silas Deane to Committee of Secret Correspondence, November
28, 1776, *New York Historical Society Collections*, vol. xix: The
Deane Papers, vol. i, New York 1887, p. 372.
[3] John Adams to John Jay, June 2, 1785, *The Diplomatic Correspondence of the United States of America from 1783 to 1789*, vol.
ii, Washington 1837, p. 371.
[4] John Adams to John Jay, December 15, 1785, *ibid.*, p. 551.

The trend toward the adoption of ceremonial and etiquette in official life received more impetus when the new federal government was inaugurated in 1789. A dignified ceremony for the meeting of the President with Congress, for the reception of foreign ministers, and for solemn political occasions seemed necessary in order to give the federal government importance and authority. Such arrangements were by no means generally popular. When John Adams, who by this time had developed into a convinced advocate of political etiquette, referred to Washington's inaugural address as "His Most Gracious Speech," he stirred a storm of indignation among the Radical members of Congress.

The connection between the establishment of the new federal government and the introduction of ceremonies in political life shows that the "ridiculous business of etiquette" formed part of a wider process: acceptance of formalized and bureaucratic methods in government. Thus, in the fifteen years which passed between the Declaration of Independence and Ternant's arrival in the United States, the administration of American foreign policy had undergone a great change. It had become more efficiently organized and, as an almost necessary consequence, diplomatic procedures were adopted similar to those used in other countries. This evolution had been slow; advances had been followed by periods of standstill and retreat. But by 1791 a bureaucratic apparatus for the conduct of diplomatic affairs was established in America.

When the Continental Congress convened in 1774, its aim was to agree on a common policy of the colonies toward Great Britain and to carry it out. The Continental Congress was, and remained, a government rather than a legislature. The preparation and supervision of the measures on which the Congress had decided were entrusted to committees composed of members of Congress. Thus, when the possibilities of reconciliation with England faded, and assistance of foreign powers for the American cause became urgent, a Committee of Secret Correspondence was formed for the purpose of handling foreign affairs. Nevertheless when particular issues arose, like the drafting of the treaty with France, a special committee was elected for this task. The disadvantages of government by Congress and its committees are obvious. Because the members were involved in a great variety of duties, committees met irregularly, and the transaction of business was slow. The simultaneous existence of several committees occupied with similar tasks—as, for instance, of the Committee of Secret Correspondence and the Committee for Drafting the Model Treaty—prevented steadiness and continuity in foreign policy. This fault was aggravated by frequent changes in the membership of the committees. Franklin, who had been the most influential member of the Committee of Secret Correspondence during the first year of its existence, had to leave it in the winter of 1776 to go to Paris. The greatest obstacle to efficient conduct of business arose from the fact that the composition of the committees mirrored the division of opinions among the members of Congress. In any significant policy decision, agreement was difficult to reach, and problems were frequently looked upon from the point of view of party advantage rather than from the point of view of their objective necessity. The opposing factions were quite uninhibited about using the knowledge which they had gained in their committee work for denunciations of their opponents. At one time the French envoy was forced to make an official complaint about the public airing of diplomatic secrets.

The methods, or lack of methods, with which foreign affairs were managed by Congress, had their repercussions in the diplomatic negotiations which the American agents were conducting in Europe. In its disregard for diplomatic customs, Congress sent out agents to all those countries where it hoped to find sympathies, and these agents were floating around in Europe because they were not received by the court to which they had been sent. The financial situation of the American agents abroad was precarious because it was expected that their expenses would be covered by the commercial business they would transact; some of the agents became deeply involved in business dealings, sometimes of a shady nature. The agents were overburdened because they had to act as "political ministers, board of admiralty, chamber of commerce, and commercial agents."[5] The main difficulty, however, was that Congress appointed not one but several agents for a single diplomatic mission, in order to reflect the differing opinions in Congress. For instance, on the mission to France, Radicals like John Adams and Arthur Lee were to counterbalance Moderates like Silas Deane.

Franklin, in a half humorous and half despairing mood, has given a graphic description of the confusion into which these methods had led: "Speaking of commissioners in the plural puts me in mind of inquiring if it can be the intention of Congress to keep *three* commissioners at this court; we have indeed four with the gentleman intended for Tuscany, who continues here, and is very angry that he was not consulted in making the treaty . . . . We shall soon have a fifth for the envoy to Vienna not being received there is, I hear, returning hither . . . . But as to our number, whatever advantage there might be in the joint councils of three for framing and adjusting the articles of the treaty, there can be none in managing the common business of a resident here. On the contrary, all the advantages in negotiation that result from secrecy of sentiment and uniformity in expressing it and in

[5] John Adams to the President of Congress, June 29, 1780, *The Revolutionary Diplomatic Correspondence of the United States*, ed. Francis Wharton, vol. IV, Washington 1889, p. 823.

common business from dispatch are lost. In a court, too, where every word is watched and weighed, if a number of commissioners do not every one hold the same language in giving their opinion on any public transaction, this lessens their weight . . . . And where every one must be consulted on every particular of common business in answering every letter, etc., and one of them is offended if the smallest thing is done without his consent, the difficulty of being often and long enough together, the different opinions and the time consumed in debating them, the interruptions by new applicants in the time of meeting, etc., occasion so much postponing and delay, that correspondence languishes, occasions are lost, and the business is always behindhand."[6]

The harm caused by this disorderly procedure in diplomatic transactions was evident to most members of the Continental Congress. Moreover, other administrative tasks—military affairs and finances—suffered from similar defects. By the end of 1776 and the beginning of 1777, some members of Congress urged the formation of executive departments headed by men who were not members of Congress and who could give their full attention to the different fields of congressional activity. The difficulty was that the attempt to achieve greater administrative efficiency was tied up with a political problem on which Congress was divided. There was a sharp conflict between those who wanted to maintain the independence and sovereignty of the single states, and those who wanted to institute a national government, thereby diminishing state autonomy. Because the creation of executive departments was regarded as an important step on the way to the establishment of a strong central government, such a measure was vehemently opposed by the Radicals who had come to control the Continental Congress in the course

[6] Benjamin Franklin to Lovell, July 22, 1778, *ibid.*, vol. II, pp. 658-659.

of 1776. Although, as convinced democrats, they had courageously fought English despotism and had been prime movers of the final break with Great Britain, they believed they could realize their democratic ideals better on a local and regional level; thus they were strong defenders of the sovereignty of the individual states. At first, the efforts toward the establishment of executive departments bore little fruit. In the spring of 1777, the Committee of Secret Correspondence was transformed into a Committee of Foreign Affairs and Thomas Paine was appointed its secretary with "a salary of 70 dollars a month"; but since this committee continued to be composed of members of Congress, the actual transaction of business was hardly improved. Only in 1780, when the Moderates regained power in Congress, were plans resumed for the organization of an executive. On January 10, 1781, Congress adopted a report creating a Department of Foreign Affairs with a Secretary of Foreign Affairs at its head. The Radicals still conducted a desperate rearguard action, but they were only able to delay the election of a Secretary of Foreign Affairs for another six months. On August 10, Robert R. Livingston was elected to this position.

Livingston was Secretary of Foreign Affairs not even two years. However, Livingston's tenure of this office was decisive in placing the conduct of American foreign affairs on a professional basis. Interference of Congress in current diplomatic business came to an end. Livingston obtained permission to correspond with the American diplomatic agents directly, independent from Congress, so that the confidential and secret nature of diplomatic business was guaranteed. Only letters concerning "great national objects" could be examined by members of Congress. Because Livingston was allowed to attend Congress to answer questions and to explain written reports, he became the main channel through which Congress was informed about diplomatic developments. Thus the Secretary of Foreign Affairs was established as the chief adviser of Congress for foreign affairs and as the executive officer in this field. Livingston was equally successful in tidying up the disorderly and chaotic situation in the American foreign service. He set up a system of graduated ranks among the American agents, and he introduced a salary scale adjusted to the importance and living costs of the country in which they served. Having provided a secure financial basis for the American agents abroad, Livingston got rid of the compromising entanglement of politics with business. Diplomatic activities were separated from consular functions, and diplomats were no longer permitted to engage in trade.

Some members of Congress resented the diminution of the influence which they could exert on the handling of foreign policy; the feeling that his work was not adequately appreciated may have contributed to Livingston's decision to give up his post. Livingston's retirement in 1783 was followed by an interregnum during which Congress and its committees directed and administered foreign affairs; accordingly there was again a lack of steady guidance and an accumulation of unanswered correspondence. But when, on May 7, 1784, the vacancy which Livingston's resignation had left was filled with the election of John Jay as Secretary of Foreign Affairs, this office quickly regained the position and authority which it had possessed under Livingston. In comparison to the luxuriously housed and numerously staffed departments of foreign affairs in the European capitals, the American foreign office was a very small establishment: in two rooms, one of which was a parlor, the Secretary, his assistant, and two clerks did their work. The existence of this office, however, demonstrated that the time of improvisations and enthusiastic experiments in American foreign policy had passed, and that an adoption of bureaucratic procedure and adjustment to traditional methods in diplomacy had taken place. The governmental reorganization, which followed from the acceptance of the Federal Constitution in 1788, then secured this development.

The construction of an efficiently functioning administrative machinery was accelerated by a growing tendency to accept traditional methods of diplomacy and foreign affairs. The first approach to France, in 1776, was inspired by the feeling that a new age was beginning, and that commercial relations, to which the Americans wanted to limit their contacts with the outside world, would supersede political connections all over the globe. In the second part of 1776, American military reserves which brought the British army down into New Jersey made the American leaders so anxious for French intervention that before the year had ended, Congress empowered its commissioners in Paris to offer the British West Indies to France as a price for participation in the war. From the high stand which Congress had taken in September of eschewing political transactions, it had, only three months later, slid to the low level of willingness to bargain about future territorial conquests. The American-French alliance, concluded in 1778, was a further significant step toward traditional diplomacy. Astonishment has frequently been expressed about the success of the American negotiators in getting their ideas accepted by Europe's most powerful monarchy. Indeed, the Treaty of Amity and Commerce between France and the United States followed closely the Model Treaty of 1776 with its new and radical principles for commerce and navigation. But, in contrast to the plan which had been drafted in 1776, and which provided only for commercial connections, the agreement made with France in 1778 included, in addition to the Treaty of Amity and Commerce, a "conditional and defensive alliance." The United States assured France of her possessions in the West

Indies, while France guaranteed the independence of America. France promised not to lay down arms before the independence of America was recognized. Neither France nor America were to conclude a separate peace, and they entered into arrangements for military cooperation. This was not a document of a "new diplomacy"; it was a political alliance pure and simple, conceived and written in the terms of old-style diplomacy.

The conclusion of a political alliance between France and America meant that the young republic, in its first contacts with the outside world, failed to realize the principles on which America had intended to base her external relations; it also meant that America was drawn into the constellations of European power politics. A close alliance existed between the two Bourbon powers of France and Spain, and France wanted to bring Spain into the war against England. To this end France promised not to make peace with England until Spain had conquered Gibraltar. Spain's military operations against Gibraltar were unsuccessful; in compensation for Spanish willingness to leave Gibraltar in England's hands, France supported Spanish claims for vast territories on the left bank of the Mississippi. Since these negotiations were conducted in secrecy, the Americans had no authentic knowledge of the diplomatic bargaining which went on between France and Spain. Congress remained full of trust in France's selfless benevolence toward America. But the American agents in Europe who had become aware of the intricacies of European diplomatic negotiations and intrigues suspected that France had made some secret arrangements over areas of vital concern to America, and that for egoistic reasons France was not interested in ending the war quickly but wanted to keep America in dependence. John Jay and John Adams, particularly, became extremely dubious about French foreign policy. In several reports, John Adams warned his countrymen against transferring the concepts of ordinary morality to the conduct of foreign affairs. No power, "not even Spain nor France, wishes to see America rise very fast to power. We ought, therefore, to be cautious how we magnify our ideas and exaggerate our expressions of the generosity and magnanimity of any of these powers."[7] Foreign policy is decided by interest alone: "The circumstances of modes, language, and religion have much less influence in determining the friendship and enmity of nations than other more essential interests."[8] Adams' experiences in Europe taught him that the idea of a natural harmony of the interests of all nations was chimerical: "When two nations have the same interests in general they are natural allies; when they have opposite interests they are natural enemies."[9] Adams also discovered the usefulness of the idea of an "equilibrium, a balance of power,"[10] which might serve to overcome the tyrannical domination of the sea which England exerted. Adams preached the need for an outlook on foreign policy which discarded idealistic illusions: "No facts are believed but decisive military conquests; no arguments are seriously attended to in Europe but force."[11] Adams became convinced that, in order to survive, America had to be well informed about the world of European diplomacy; "I think it our indispensable duty, as it is our undoubted right, to send ministers to other courts and endeavor to extend our acquaintance, commerce and political connexions with all the world."[12]

[7] John Adams to the President of Congress, April 18, 1780, *ibid.*, vol. iii, p. 623.

[8] John Adams to Genêt, May 17, 1780, *ibid.*, p. 687.

[9] *Ibid.*, pp. 685-686.

[10] John Adams to the President of Congress, March 12, 1780, *ibid.*, p. 542.

[11] John Adams to Benjamin Franklin, August 17, 1780, *ibid.*, vol. iv, p. 35.

[12] John Adams to Robert R. Livingston, September 6, 1782, *ibid.*, vol. v, p. 704.

Livingston, to whom this letter was addressed, must have been sympathetic to this advice. When he had become Secretary of Foreign Affairs, he instructed the American agents in Europe to report to him "minutely everything that can in any way to be of use to us." He demanded to get "minutiae . . . since nothing short of this can give us a just idea of our foreign politics."[13] Thus the establishment of close political relations with France and, consequently, with European politics in general modified the original American contempt for diplomacy and power politics. Exact knowledge of the way in which European power politics functioned, and continuous observation of the European political scene was recognized as necessary. Soon old-style diplomacy was even practiced; for in a move which could hardly be criticized by diplomats of the *ancien régime* but which was less becoming to the advocates of a new political ethic, the American agents signed the preliminaries of the peace with England without previously informing their French ally, thereby violating the terms of the alliance treaty between France and America.

The conclusion of peace seemed to make possible a return to the idealistic principles with which America had entered the field of foreign policy. Traditional diplomacy and power politics seemed to be elements of a past epoch. But it was not accidental that this return to the principles of the Model Treaty occurred in the time of the interregnum between the secretaryships of Livingston and Jay, when Congress had resumed the administration of foreign affairs. With Jay at the helm, the course of American foreign policy again became more practical and realistic. The peace represented less the beginning of a new era than it might have appeared in the first flush of enthusiasm. The new republic was not the only power on the North American continent, but was surrounded by great European powers—by England in the

[13] Robert R. Livingston to John Adams, May 30, 1782, *ibid.*, p. 460.

north, and Spain in the south and west—whose boundaries with America were still in dispute. The most valuable and necessary markets for America—Great Britain and the British West Indies—were still closed to American trade. Even France, with which a liberal commercial treaty was in force, maintained a tobacco monopoly and thus prevented the free flow of commerce in one of America's most important products for export. As John Adams wrote, France had conceded to America not a truly liberal system of commerce but "an artful appearance of it"; he doubted that "monopoly, prohibition, exclusion, and navigation acts, will be abolished so soon as some speculators imagine."[14] Would it also be necessary for America to subordinate commerce to political ends, to use trade for achieving favorable agreements with individual powers, and to adopt a policy of prohibitions and exclusions? This question, which would hardly have been raised in the first years of American independence, was seriously debated in the 1780's. This change in attitude is reflected in a letter from Jay to Jefferson: "The spirit of monopoly and exclusion has prevailed in Europe too long to be done away at once; and however enlightened the present age may appear when compared with former ones, yet, whenever ancient prejudices are touched, we find that we only have light enough to see our want of more. Toleration in commerce, like toleration in religion, gains ground, it is true; but I am not sanguine in my expectations that either will soon take place in their due extent."[15]

In the Federal Convention of 1787, James Madison once spoke of the developments which had led to American independence. One might have expected him to explain that it was a triumph of freedom over tyranny, of the forces of the

[14] John Adams to John Jay, August 29, 1785, *The Diplomatic Correspondence of the United States of America from 1783 to 1789*, vol. II, p. 464.
[15] April 24, 1788, *ibid.*, p. 141.

future over those of the past. It is characteristic of the increasing importance which considerations of power politics had gained that, in Madison's opinion, it was to the principle of the rivalry between England and France that "we owe perhaps our liberty."[16]

Americans might still dislike traditional diplomacy and power politics, but they no longer viewed them as feeble structures which would fall at the first blowing of the trumpets of liberty. Americans had become aware that, behind the forms of foreign policy and diplomacy as they existed in Europe, there lay a coherent system of thought, of principles, of methods. They had begun to use its terms and to think in its concepts. The ideas which stood behind the European diplomatic practice were a further influence in the formation of the American outlook on foreign affairs.

II

In the eighteenth century diplomacy attained its full maturity; diplomatic forms and institutions took the shape which they have preserved into the present time. Justifiedly, the eighteenth century has been called the "classical age of diplomacy." With the conclusion of the Thirty Years' War in the middle of the seventeenth century, religious wars came to an end. No longer did autonomous and sovereign states need to conceal or twist their pursuit of political aims by the pretense of striving for the re-establishment of Christian unity in the Western World. Nationalism, which again made foreign policy serve the purposes of higher values, came only with the nineteenth century. The eighteenth century, more than the preceding or the following one, was an era of "pure politics" entirely dominated by the concept of power. Frederick the Great expressed the spirit of the politics of his age

[16] June 28, 1787, *The Records of the Federal Convention of 1787*, ed. Max Farrand, vol. i, New Haven 1911, p. 448.

when he wrote that "the permanent principle of rulers is to extend as far as their power permits them."[17]

Although in the eighteenth century many voices, some of them brilliant and penetrating, criticized and opposed the uninhibited exercise of power politics, the fact remains that they had a very limited effect on the political practice of the time. In England, where the bourgeoisie was gradually rising into the ruling group, the conduct of foreign policy might have been somewhat tempered by the critics of power politics. On the European Continent, where a feudal and agrarian ruling class was still in exclusive control—embattled in France, almost undisputed in Central and Eastern Europe—naked power politics with the aim of the widest possible territorial expansion not only was pursued but also was regarded as the legitimate purpose of foreign policy. Maneuvering for aggrandizement even found a greater scope in the eighteenth century because of the shifting political constellations, because of the disappearance of old political contrasts and the emergence of new ones. Russia conquered Lithuania and Esthonia from Sweden and destroyed the independence of Courland. Austria swept over Hungary into Serbia and Bosnia and, together with Russia, aspired to the establishment of a Christian empire in Constantinople. Prussia grabbed Silesia from Austria and plotted to annex Saxony. Spain stretched out for Sardinia and Sicily. Those states that were too weak to take the initiative were overrun, or else they had to rely for protection on an alliance with a stronger power and submit to its commands. Stanislas Lesczynski, the King of Poland, was moved to Lorraine, while the ruling family of Lorraine was transplanted to Tuscany so that France could round off her territories in the west, and

[17] Friedrich II, der Grosse, of Prussia, "Considérations sur l'état présent du Corps Politique de l'Europe," in Frédéric le Grand, *Oeuvres*, vol. VIII, Berlin 1848, p. 15.

Austria could tighten her hold on Italy. Joseph II of Hapsburg stirred up a diplomatic crisis by his project to give the
Netherlands to the Dukes of Bavaria, while Bavaria would be
annexed to neighboring Austria. This scramble for territorial
expansion at the expense of the weaker reached its climax at
the end of the eighteenth century in the partition of Poland
when the "three crowned sinners," as the indignant Bentham
called the rulers of Russia, Austria, and Prussia, erased the
fourth largest state of Europe from the political map.

Brutality in methods corresponded to ruthlessness in aims.
Alliances, hastily made, were quickly abandoned when their
usefulness was exhausted. England withdrew from the War
of the Spanish Succession when the goals which she had pursued in forging the great alliance against France had been
achieved; thus England left her coalition partners to fend for
themselves. Frederick II of Prussia entered the War of the
Austrian Succession as an ally of the French, but twice in the
course of the war he deserted them and concluded a separate
peace with Austria. At the end of the century, in the War of
Coalition against the French Revolution, Prussia suddenly
made peace when her commitment in the west denied her
the chance to pursue conquests in the east. Disregard for
treaty obligations or sudden change of sides involved no
moral opprobrium or loss of prestige. "One must regard as
a fundamental maxim and incontestable principle," wrote
a French diplomat, "that the reputation and prestige of a
prince or of any state, his dignity and importance, his rank
in the political world is necessarily based on power."[18]

All the various tasks of government were geared to the
requirements of power politics. The center of attention was
the army. Economic policy was subordinated to military
purposes. The government promoted those manufactures

[18] [Favier], *Politique de tous les cabinets de l'Europe*, vol. i, Paris
1793, p. 191.

which would serve the needs of the army; by restricting imports and furthering exports, a favorable balance of trade was to be created which would permit the maintenance of and, if possible, the increase of a powerful military establishment. Next to the army and finances, foreign policy was the ruler's great concern. Again Frederick the Great has given a striking formulation to the policy of subordinating all government activities to power politics: "Finances, foreign policy and army cannot be separated; they must be guided neck and neck like the horses drawing the Olympic chariots, which, advancing with equal strength and in the same step, quickly race over the prescribed course to the goal, and crown their driver with victory."[19]

But power politics, undisguised and untrammeled by moral values and higher aims, was only one factor which made the eighteenth century the "classical age of diplomacy." The other was supplied by the intellectual climate of the period, by its scientific and systematizing spirit. The world was believed to be controlled by laws. After Newton's great discoveries which had revealed the laws ruling the physical universe, interest focused on finding those which would determine social life. Thus even the power struggle among states was considered to have its laws. The attempt to discover these laws, though condemned to futility because of an erroneous belief in the rationality of human society, resulted in a clearer insight into the nature of diplomacy and in a sharper definition of its tasks.

It was characteristic that the terms "diplomacy" and "diplomats" as designations for the business of foreign policy and for those who transact it came into use in the eighteenth century. Previously, the broad term "politique" included foreign policy, and the men who conducted its negotiations

[19] Friedrich der Grosse, *Politische Korrespondenz*, Ergaenzungsband: *Die Politischen Testamente Friedrichs des Grossen*, ed. G. B. Volz, Berlin 1920, pp. 77-78.

had a number of different names, such as "minister" or "plenipotentiary" or "ambassador." However, the search for the laws determining social life required definition and distinction of man's manifold social activities.

The attempt to separate the conduct of foreign policy from other political activities, from which the adoption of the term "diplomacy" arose, had the consequence that diplomatic activity was thought to need a suitable equipment of its own. Diplomacy was no longer regarded as a job which amateurs, versatile generals, or amiable courtiers could pursue successfully; it became a profession demanding special training and intensive preparation. "If you could establish as a definite and permanent rule to entrust in France negotiations only to those who have gone through a period of training and studies . . . like it has been established as a constant rule to give command over armies only to those who have gained experience in several campaigns, it is clear that the king would be better served in the conduct of foreign affairs."[20]

A number of schools for the training of diplomats were instituted in the eighteenth century. The first one was the "Academy of Politics" which Torcy, the French Foreign Secretary, established in 1712 in the Louvre, where six well-born and wealthy young men received instruction twice a week "in all the sciences needed for the diplomatic profession."[21] Twelve years later, England followed the French example. It had been represented to George I that he should have "a constant supply of Persons every Way qualified for the Management of such weighty affairs and negotiations as Your Majesties Occasions may require."[22] Thus the King provided

[20] From chapter v on "des connoissances nécessaires et utiles à un négociateur," in De Callières, *De la Manière de Négocier avec les Souverains*, Brussels 1716, p. 51.

[21] After the description in De Flassan, *Histoire générale et raisonnée de la Diplomatie française*, 2nd edition, vol. IV, Paris 1811, p. 413.

[22] *Endowments of the University of Cambridge*, ed. John Willis Clark, Cambridge 1904, pp. 185, 187.

scholarships in Oxford and Cambridge so that a few young men would be taught modern languages, international law, and modern history under the tutorship of two persons "of sober conversation and prudent conduct" for whom new professorships were endowed. This was the modest beginning of the famous Regius Professorships of Modern History in Oxford and Cambridge. Prussia adopted measures similar to those of the two great Western powers. Frederick the Great installed a seminar for future diplomats where twelve young men with the title of "Legationsrat" worked as apprentices under the eyes of the cabinet ministers.[23] In the latter half of the eighteenth century, the best reputed training school for diplomats on the Continent was directed by two University of Strassburg professors, Schoepflin and Koch; among their students were Talleyrand, Metternich, and Benjamin Constant—significant proof of the impact of the "classical age of diplomacy" on later times.

What a diplomat of the eighteenth century was expected to do can be learned from the great number of books written to provide diplomats with the knowledge necessary for the exercise of their profession. Favorite topics, of course, were etiquette and the external forms of diplomatic life; the two most famous books on this subject, by Wicquefort and Callières, were published in 1681 and in 1716 and ran through many editions in the eighteenth century. The writers of this time were quite as conscious, however, as we are, that correct appearance and behavior were only presuppositions for success in diplomacy. The main business of a diplomat was "treaty-making" and "the art of negotiation." The term "diplomacy" reflects this view; the word was derived from a collection of treaties and official documents which Leibniz had published in 1695 under the title *Codex juris gentium diplomaticus*, and in which the word "diploma" was used in

[23] Friedrich der Grosse, *Politischen Testamente*, p. 54.

a broader sense than in its original meaning of "charter." Treaties were looked upon as the chief purpose and product of diplomacy. Many collections of treaties, alliances, and agreements were published in the eighteenth century. Jenkinson's *Collection of all the treaties of peace, alliance and commerce between Great Britain and other powers,* the eight folio volumes of Dumont's *Corps universel diplomatique du droit des gens,* and Martens' *Recueil des Traités,* which was continued into the twentieth century, are still of use.

The emphasis placed on treaties and treaty-making implied a recognition of the role of power in foreign policy. Instead of an all-comprehensive international law which contained the answer to any problem which might arise in the relations among states, concrete settlements, established by power politics and fixed in individual treaties, were regarded to be the complex juridical background of international relations. The shift from a system of law to a system of power was indicated by Dumont when, in the introduction of his *Corps universel diplomatique,* he wrote that this work would serve not only to justify the rights and claims of princes but also to show their "interests."

"Interest" was a crucial concept in the discussions on foreign affairs and diplomacy in the eighteenth century. "Interest" appeared to offer the key to an understanding of the laws which ruled in foreign policy. In characterizing "interest" as the driving force in foreign policy, the fact of a continuous striving for greater power and expansion was acknowledged, but, at the same time, an analysis of the concept of "interest" seemed to suggest the possibility of discovering rules and a system behind the apparent anarchy of power politics. Writers on the role and nature of "interest" in foreign policy were considered as the true "experts" of diplomacy. They formed what has been called the school of the "doctrine of the interests of the states."

These writers coolly acknowledged that a brutal struggle for power determined the relationship between states. Each state would expand until its advances were halted by counter-pressure. If the world was not in a permanent state of war, the reason was that one force found itself confronted by another force of equal strength. Whereas idealists and reformers inveighed against the idea of balance of power, the realistic writers on the doctrine of the interests of the states were its enthusiastic advocates; it appeared to them as the one stabilizing factor in a constantly moving world. The aim of diplomacy was to evaluate correctly the interplay of opposing forces and interests and to create a constellation favorable to conquest and expansion. How was it possible to make calculations with any degree of certainty in this anarchy of power politics? The writers on the interests of the states believed themselves in possession of the thread which could guide the statesmen through the labyrinth of power politics. In their view, the nature of the interest of each state could be analyzed and formulated; it could be summed up in a definite rule, a maxim.

As the term "true interest" indicates, one of the possible pitfalls was to misjudge the true interest because of deception by "imaginary" or "apparent" interests. Rulers who followed their whims or chased after prestige placed the "imaginary" or "apparent" interest over the "true" interest. But while it was relatively easy to show what ought to be avoided, the crux of the matter lay in determining the factors which composed the "true interest."

Some of these fundamental factors were pointed out by Pufendorf and Bolingbroke. Although both had a much wider outlook than the typical writers of the school on the interests of the states, they were very close to them in their ideas on foreign policy. Pufendorf and Bolingbroke refined the concept of "true interest" by separating permanent from temporary interest. Bolingbroke described the elements which formed the permanent interest of a state: "the situation of countries, the character of people, the nature of government and even that of climate and soil."[24] Pufendorf held very similar views. According to him the perpetual interest "depends chiefly on the Situation and Constitution of the Country and the natural Inclinations of the people."[25] While these factors must be assumed to be static, the temporary interest was established by "the Condition, Strength, and Weakness of the neighboring Nations." These ideas provided the point of departure for the typical writers of the school, like Courtilz de Sandras, Rousset, Favier, and Peyssonel. While the net of rational categories in which Pufendorf and Bolingbroke had tried to catch the slippery concept of the true interest of the state had been rather wide-meshed, these publicists sought to make it more tightly woven. Constitutional forms and geographical conditions remained fundamental considerations, but others were added: size and population of a state, its chief economic activities, its military organization and strength. Thus a great number of variations became possible. The true interest of a large commercial monarchy would be different from that of a large agrarian monarchy, but also from that of a small commercial monarchy or a commercial republic. The interest of each European power was deduced from an analysis in which all the factors fitting the particular case were taken into account. Then the line of policy which each state ought to follow, its "permanent *maxim d'état*," could be established. Success in foreign policy, these writers believed, depended on strict adherence to an explicitly defined system of policy based on a clear conception of a state's "true interest." "Each state must form a

[24] Bolingbroke, "The Idea of a Patriot King," in Bolingbroke, *Works*, vol. III, Dublin 1793, p. 102.

[25] From the Preface of Samuel Pufendorf, *An Introduction to the History of the Principal Kingdoms and States of Europe*, London 1766.

rational system of policy which it must follow constantly."[26]

The books on the interests of the states are dull reading. Their scheme of organization was explained by Rousset: "I treat the politics and the interests of each state in isolation, and as if I had to treat with that state alone. In another chapter I treat in the same way the politics and interests of another state, pursuing the maxims and habits of that state as if I had to treat no other. This plan could be executed without contradiction because the interests of one state are almost necessarily always in contradiction and opposition with those of another."[27] Rousset may be right in saying that this scheme is not contradictory, but it is certainly repetitive and monotonous. In a chapter on England, the relations between England and Spain are treated from the English point of view. In the chapter on Spain, the same topic is dealt with, this time from the Spanish angle. Tedious as this method is, it is effective in showing the advantages of a centrally directed and coherent foreign policy in which the relation to each individual state, and in which every single action, forms part of a conscious pattern.

By dealing with each state in isolation, Europe was artificially torn into parts; the interconnected nature of the European state system, in which the move of one member affected all others, was not recognized. That is the obvious criticism which can be raised against these writings. But in their defense it might be said that it was difficult for practical politicians to become aware of the slow and gradual development of a European state system because the policy toward economic autarchy which the governments pursued had the appearance of restricting contacts and of

[26] Article "Système Politique" in Demeunier, "Économie Politique et Diplomatique," vol. IV, Paris 1788, p. 313, in *Encyclopédie Méthodique*.

[27] Jean Rousset de Missy, *Recueil Historique d'Actes, Négociations, Mémoires et Traitez*, vol. XI, Amsterdam 1746, pp. 3-4.

closing off each state from its neighbor. Moreover, the writers of the school of the interests of the states did not really consider each European state an entirely autonomous unit, able to mould its independent system of foreign policy. They made a sharp distinction between great and small states and emphasized that the maxim which ought to govern the foreign policy of a great power must differ from the principles which a small state had to follow, because the latter could not have an independent system of policy. In the eyes of these writers, there were only a limited number of political systems in Europe, each of them grouped around a great power.

The climate of opinion created by the scientific discoveries of the age can be discerned in the views of these writers about the way in which each great power fashioned its policy. Swift has immortalized the mathematical craze of the period by his description of the people of Laputa who could enjoy their food only if it was offered to them in the shape of a geometrical figure. The belief of the writers on the interests of the states in the possibility of measuring precisely the power of a state—according to its size, population, and income—reflected something of this mathematical fad. Newton's influence is also noticeable; some of these writers were anxious to present their views in terms of Newtonian concepts and principles. The individual state would be called a gravitation center which formed a system by attracting smaller states; these "move in the orbit" of the larger power. Like planets, the great powers would take their own course, sweeping in their wake a number of satellites. The great powers would be kept within a calculable orbit because they would meet other systems which they were not strong enough to attract, but strong enough to resist. Although the intention of these writers was to discuss the policy of every European state, they devoted their main efforts to an analysis of the policy of the great powers which were masters of their own fortune, capable of forming their own system of policy.

The doctrine of the interests of the states was set forth not only in books surveying the entire European political scene; this way of thinking also dominated another type of political literature: Political Testaments. The affinity between the Political Testaments and the doctrine of the interests of the states can be seen from an article on "Political Systems" in the *Encyclopédie Méthodique.* The author stated that it is not enough that the system of foreign policy "is in the head of the sovereign or of the ministers, it must be set down in writing." This document should then be "placed in the archives among the most important secrets of the state, so that it can serve as a guide to those leaders who will come later."[28] This is exactly what the writers of Political Testaments intended to achieve. Because they contained an analysis of the policy of only one country, the Political Testaments permitted a subtle and detailed application of the doctrine of the interests of the states. Moreover, they show the intimate connection existing between the writers of this school and the practical politicians. Some of the Political Testaments were inventions, composed by literary men who, by claiming to publish the last will of a well-known statesman, presented a thorough statement of the policy of a single country from the point of view of the doctrine of the interests of the states. Others, however, were authentic, the work of a leading minister or a prince who tried to explain the principles which had guided his policy and which he wanted his successor to continue. There was hardly an important ruler or statesman in the eighteenth century whose death was not followed by the publication of his Political Testament.

Among the many Political Testaments of the eighteenth century, one stands out beyond all others. The apogee of this

[28] Demeunier, *op.cit.*, vol. iv, p. 313.

genre was reached with the Political Testament of Frederick II of Prussia, the most eminent ruler in the Age of Enlightenment, "the Great King," "the philosopher of Sanssouci." In his political actions Frederick tried to be guided by philosophy and scientific principles. His first Political Testament was written in 1752 at a fortunate moment in his career. In two short campaigns he had conquered Silesia from Austria, but he had not yet fought the destructive Seven Years' War against the coalition of Austria, France, and Russia. Proud of his achievements Frederick wanted to give his successor "information about what experience had taught me like a pilot who knows the stormy passages of the political ocean. I want to indicate the rocks which must be avoided, the ports where refuge can be found."[29] Frederick insisted that a ruler ought to realize that "a well organized government needs to have a system which is as closely knit as a philosophical system, all its measures must be well thought out, and finances, administration and army must be directed toward the same aim, namely the strengthening of the state and the increase of its power."[30] Consequently, Frederick described the whole governmental organization of Prussia: the judicial system, financial resources, internal administration, and military organization. But the centerpiece of Frederick's Political Testament was the long section on Prussia's foreign policy.

The terminology and the concepts of this discussion reveal Frederick's indebtedness to the doctrine of the interests of the state. Emphasis on the idea of "balance of power," the distinction of "true" and "permanent" interests from temporary motives like vanity and thirst for fame, the search for maxims—all these elements of Frederick's analysis show his acceptance of the tenets of the school and his complete agreement with its methods. Frederick's recommendations for

[29] Friedrich der Grosse, *Politischen Testamente*, p. 1.
[30] *Ibid.*, p. 38.

Prussia's foreign policy were preceded by a precisely detailed survey of the interests of the other European states. Frederick was aware of the differences in political interests between great and small states; his chief concern were the four great European powers: France, England, Austria, and Russia. France's dominant aim was to weaken England, Austria's to regain Silesia, Russia's to control Poland. These facts had to be taken for granted in charting Prussia's course. Because Austria's hostility toward Prussia could not be overcome, the latter would have to seek protection by means of an alliance with Russia which had no permanent conflicts of interest with Prussia. Such a policy might offer a chance of attaining what ought to be Prussia's next goals: an *arrondissement* of Prussian territory by the annexation of Saxony and by the acquisition of the Polish area which separated East Prussia from the other lands of the Prussian King.

Whereas the writers on the interests of the states tried to be explicit in the maxims they deduced from the "true" interests of the states, Frederick's recommendations for Prussia's foreign policy were flexible and tentative. By analyzing the permanent factors in the policies of the great powers, Frederick hoped to remove chance and uncertainty from foreign affairs; but his practical political experience had cautioned him against exclusive reliance on such considerations and had made him aware of the importance of personal and temporary elements. Frederick indicated that whatever the internal strength and the permanent interests of France, the financial difficulties resulting from the wastefulness of Louis XV would immobilize France in the coming years. It seemed likely to him that English foreign policy could not remain uninfluenced by domestic developments, the brewing conflict between King and Parties. Frederick warned his successors against planning far ahead because "politics is subjected to many accidents."[31] It was impossible to define Prussia's future foreign policy more exactly. The best advice which Frederick could give was to "wait for opportunities" and "to profit from favourable circumstances."[32]

This vagueness was humiliating to the "philosopher-king." In 1768, after the Seven Years' War, which had wrought so many changes, Frederick composed another Political Testament, but he arrived at a no more definite conclusion than he had previously. Then he continued to struggle with the problem in a number of memoranda, designed to instruct his successor. Again Frederick could give no more substantial advice, but he indicated what seemed to him a satisfactory explanation of his failure to present a concrete program for Prussia's foreign policy. Because Prussia was a growing state, insecure in its present territorial setting, its interests had not taken on a permanent shape; Prussia's rulers had to be watchful and to rely on changing constellations. Frederick could formulate no more positive maxim than that opportunism was the appropriate attitude for Prussian foreign policy.

This reasoning seems superficial. It is nearer to the truth to say that the view of politics which Frederick had gained as the ruler of an important state was incompatible with the rigid and mechanistic concepts underlying the doctrine of the interests of the states; the dynamic forces which work continuously in political life cannot be pressed into the Procrustean bed of permanent maxims and formulas.

Nevertheless, the doctrine of the interests of the states had value. Divested of its rationalistic exaggerations, the doctrine of the interests of the states contained a kernel of truth and opened a new vista for an understanding of the developments of history. After the Middle Ages to which the domination of Christian values had given an organizing principle, the suc-

[31] *Ibid.*, p. 58.
[32] *Ibid.*, pp. 59, 62.

ceeding centuries had appeared to be a conglomeration of arbitrariness and accidents. In maintaining that the policy of each state was based on permanent interests, a thread was provided through which the history of Europe since the end of the fifteenth century became a causally connected whole. In the preface to his *History of the Reign of the Emperor Charles V*, William Robertson, the eighteenth-century Scotch historian, wrote that the importance of the reign of Charles V lay in the fact that "the powers of Europe were formed into one great political system, in which each took a station, wherein it has since remained . . . . The great events which happened then have not hitherto spent their force. The political principles and maxims, then established, still continue to operate. The ideas concerning the balance of power, then introduced, still influence the councils of nations." In this manner the doctrine of the interests of the states has become an integral part of modern diplomatic history.

III

The eighteenth-century concepts of diplomacy were important because they show the way of thinking which Americans encountered and absorbed when they tried to establish America as an independent state. This body of thought had significance for the beginnings of American foreign policy in still another way. America had been an issue of diplomatic discussions; they had prepared a place for America in the international state system.

Two diametrically opposed trends of thought regarding America's role in foreign policy can be distinguished. One was that the happenings in the colonial sphere could be entirely separated from the contentions in the European world. The other was that the economic importance of colonial possessions exerted a decisive influence on the

European balance of power; colonies became the main objects of the rivalries among the European states.

The first notion—that the European sphere and the colonial sphere could be kept apart—can be traced back to the sixteenth century. When, in 1559, France and Spain tried to end the long struggle which had begun with the French invasion of Italy in 1494, their diplomatic negotiators were able to agree on a settlement of the outstanding European questions, but their conflicting aims on the American continent seemed to form a stumbling block. Neither power had a clear idea of the extent of the territories and treasures involved and each was unwilling to make concessions, not knowing what riches it abandoned by lowering its claims. Thus when the peace treaty was signed, it contained no provisions about colonies. This led to the elaboration of a principle which, in the following decades, became a recognized doctrine of international law: that peace in Europe did not mean that there was also peace "beyond the line" which divided Europe from America. In the seventeenth century the principle itself remained in force, but its meaning became reversed. The reason was a change in the political constellation. France, occupied with her quest for European hegemony, had to concentrate all her forces on the European Continent. Spain and Portugal were in retreat before the Netherlands and England, which, with youthful energy, had entered the race for colonies on the American continent. It became of vital interest to the Catholic powers to maintain the status quo in America and to separate the situation in the American colonies from the changing fortunes of the European wars. Peace "beyond the line," while there was war in Europe, became their aim. The concept of neutrality, which had just been introduced into international law, served as a useful instrument for such purposes. Various treaties concluded between France and England provided for the neutralization of the colonies in the case of a European conflict; the most important was the one of 1686 between Louis XIV and James II, which, as we have seen, became ninety years later a model for the American draft treaty of 1776.

After the treaty of 1686, the tendency towards effecting a separation of the European and American sphere by diplomatic agreements and international law lingered on in diplomatic negotiations and discussions, but statesmen became increasingly aware of the decisive importance which colonial possessions had for the weight which a state could throw into the European balance of power. "The balance of commerce of the nations in America is like the balance of power in Europe. One must add that these two balances are actually one. Commerce forms the strength of states, and a country which emphasizes commerce will always be able to make the scale of the balance of power come down on its side."[33] More than others, Frenchmen became obsessed with this idea. They needed an explanation for the steady decline of their influence in Europe throughout the eighteenth century, and they believed that they had found the explanation in the fact that in the settlement which, in 1715, ended the War of the Spanish Succession the French statesmen had miscalculated the weight of the colonial factor. The peace treaties of 1715 had loaded the balance of power against France. Commerce and colonies came to be regarded as the pivot of the balance of power. "The true balance of power really resides in commerce and in America," the French Foreign Minister Choiseul wrote in 1759,[34] and Vergennes justified his policy to support the American colonies against the English with considerations of the balance of power. American independ-

[33] J. N. Moreau, *Mémoire pour servir à l'histoire de notre tems*, vol. I, Frankfurt 1757, p. 4.
[34] De Flassan, *op.cit.*, vol. VI, p. 160.

ence would take away a "considerable weight in the balance of power."[35]

Thus the separation of the American colonies from the British Empire, and the setting up of an independent state on the American continent was an event which, from the point of view of the prevailing diplomatic thinking, must have far-reaching repercussions on the entire European situation. On which side would the weight of the new republic be thrown? Would American independence upset the European balance of power? But the ideas about the place of America, which had found expression in the treaties of the sixteenth and seventeenth centuries, suggested as a further possibility that America could remain outside the systems of the great European powers and form a gravitation center of her own. These earlier ideas could serve to determine the role of America in the international world.

It is not clear to what extent the majority of American diplomats were aware of these earlier treaties and the views about the separation of the European and American spheres which they contained. But Americans were deeply interested and impressed by a pamphlet which appeared in England during the War of Independence and in which these ideas were revived. The pamphlet bore the title "A Memorial to the Sovereigns of Europe." It represented a curious mixture of different intellectual trends; it contained a strongly idealistic element, but it was couched in the terms and concepts of the doctrine of the interests of the states. The author of this pamphlet was Thomas Pownall. When it was published in 1780, Pownall was an outsider in British politics, a defender of radical and unpopular causes. His tendencies towards extremism and contrariness may have been increased because after a promising beginning in a government career, he had

[35] Henri Doniol, *Histoire de la Participation de la France à l'Établissement des États-Unis d'Amerique*, vol. i, Paris 1886, p. 243.

received no further political preference and spent most of his life in impotent opposition. But his experiences in the British government had given him a unique insight into American affairs and they always remained in the center of his interests. Pownall had served as an English officer in the Seven Years' War, and then he became Governor of Massachusetts. While he was in America he had taken part in the Congress of Albany when the needs of defense had given rise to the drafting of a plan for union. Since then, Pownall was haunted by the idea that such a union might take place outside the British Empire. When, in 1764, he wrote his famous work, *Administration of the British Colonies,* he suggested the plan of a British union, in which the colonists would receive representation in the House of Commons. He feared that without a reform of this kind, Great Britain might cease "to be the center of attraction to which these colonies must tend."[36] Almost prophetically, he envisaged the possibility that "by attraction amongst themselves," the colonies might draw together in "an American union."[37] When the war had broken out and the colonists had asked for and received French support, Pownall had no illusion that the previous situation could ever be restored. In 1777 he declared in the House of Commons, "A people, whose affairs are interwoven and so connected as the affairs of the Americans are with several European states, pledging themselves to those states in this solemn manner, are engaged beyond all possibility of retreat . . . ."[38]

In his *Memorial . . . to the Sovereigns of Europe,* written while the War of Independence was still going on, Pownall took it for granted that "the independence of America is fixed

[36] Thomas Pownall, *Administration of the British Colonies,* vol. i, London 1774, p. 40.

[37] *Ibid.,* vol. ii, p. 84.

[38] December 2, 1777, see Cobbett's *Parliamentary History of England,* vol. xix, p. 526.

as fate; she is mistress of her own fortune."[39] "This new system of power," he stated, "united in and moving round its own proper center . . . is growing, by accellerated notions, and accumulated accretion of parts, into an independent organized being, a great and powerful empire. It has taken its equal station with the nations upon earth."[40] Since Pownall regarded American independence as accomplished, his task in the *Memorial* was to probe into the consequences. In a language which combined the diplomatic terminology of the period with Newtonian concepts, Pownall stated: "North America is become a new primary planet in the system of the world, which while it takes its own course, in its own orbit, must have effect on the orbit of every other planet, and shift the common center of gravity of the whole system of the European world." In outlining what seemed to him the most desirable future course for America, Pownall relied heavily on Paine's *Common Sense*, which he quoted at length. America should reap the advantages of the situation, "removed from the old world, and all its embroiled interests and wrangling politics, without an enemy or a rival, or the entanglement of alliances."[41] America's real connection with Europe should be purely commercial and she should become a free port for all European nations. Pownall painted a brilliant picture of America's future if such a policy would be followed. She will "become the Arbitress of the commercial [world] and perhaps the Mediatrix of peace, and of the political business of the world." Pownall was convinced that the South American colonies too would sever their bonds with Europe. If America conducted her policy intelligently and made clever use of the rivalries between the European powers, she should be able to acquire hegemony over the entire

---

[39] [Thomas Pownall], *A Memorial most humbly addressed to the Sovereigns of Europe*, London 1780, p. 5.
[40] *Ibid.*, pp. 3-4.
[41] *Ibid.*, pp. 77-78.

continent. "The whole of the Spanish, Dutch, Danish, French and British establishments . . . must in the course of events become parts as of the communion, so of the great North American dominion, established on the basis of that union."[42]

Pownall's use of Paine's *Common Sense* suggests that he was susceptible to the reform idealism of the eighteenth century. But his acceptance of these views was only partial. Pownall did not believe that America's separation from the European state system would usher in a new age of peace.

It might be possible for America to withdraw from European power politics, but she would have to live according to the rules of power politics in her own system, the American sphere. Probably Pownall's ideas for the American future were somewhat inspired by English patriotism; if Britain was unable to control the North American colonies, it was in the English interest that the colonies should not line up with France or another European power and place their weight in the balance against England.

As a friend of the American cause, Pownall would have been carefully listened to, and his ideas would have been greatly valued by the Americans under all circumstances. But it is evident that, for the Americans, the significance of his pamphlet must have been heightened by the apparent closeness of its views to Paine's *Common Sense*. Pownall's pamphlet built a bridge between the political idealism of the first years of independence and the realistic evaluation of traditional power factors which the Americans were forced to accept. Certainly John Adams was deeply impressed by Pownall's pamphlet. He immediately had it translated into French and sent to all those in Europe whose views on America could be important. Thus Pownall's *Memorial* became an official American propaganda piece. There is something ironic in the fact that a treatise imbued with the spirit of the

[42] *Ibid.*, p. 18.

school of the interests of the states was the first programmatic exposition of American foreign policy with which the diplomats of the struggling young republic appealed to the Europeans of the *ancien régime*.

IV

Although many Americans looked upon the prospect of participating in power politics only with horror or acknowledged the necessity of such a policy only with reservations and hesitations, eighteenth-century power politics had an effective advocate on the American continent. It spoke authoritatively and decisively through the voice of Alexander Hamilton.

Domineering, arrogant, aristocratic, and convinced of an élite's right to political leadership, Hamilton tended by inclination to power politics. In *The Farmer Refuted* of 1774—the pamphlet which he wrote when he was seventeen and with which he took his share in the defense of the American cause against British tyranny—he sounded a more practical note than the other participants in the debate on American rights. Remarks that "the promises of princes and statesmen are of little weight,"[43] or categoric statements that "deplorable is the condition of that people who have nothing else than the wisdom and justice of another to depend upon,"[44] show the realistic and skeptical mind of the young Hamilton. This natural bent towards power politics was strengthened by study. A list of his readings from the year 1778 shows his acquaintance with works from the school of the interests of the states; among others it contains the works of Frederick the Great and Robertson.

It was not until 1787, however, that Hamilton made a

[43] Hamilton, "The Farmer Refuted," in Alexander Hamilton, *Works*, ed. Henry Cabot Lodge, vol. i, New York 1904, p. 169.
[44] *Ibid.*, p. 73.

comprehensive statement on foreign policy. When he spoke at that time in the Federal Convention, he showed that he had given much thought to the problems of foreign policy and had formed definite and—in the American atmosphere—unpopular views about them. Hamilton's words were like cold water on all those idealistic ideas which had been so popular in the first years of independence. According to Hamilton, there was no possibility of escaping from power politics: "You have to protect your rights against Canada in the north, Spain in the south, and your western frontier against the savages." There ought to be no reliance on commerce as a guarantee of peace: "Jealousy of commerce as well as jealousy of power begets war." Hamilton summarized his views in the striking passage: "It had been said that respectability in the eyes of foreign Nations was not the object at which we aimed; that the proper object of republican Government was domestic tranquillity and happiness. This was an ideal distinction. No Government could give us tranquillity and happiness at home, which did not possess sufficient stability and strength to make us respectable abroad."[45]

These ideas were elaborated by Hamilton in the *Federalist*. The section on foreign policy represented a frontal attack on utopianism in foreign policy. Hamilton was undoubtedly aware of the strength of this attitude in America. He vigorously refuted the opinion that "permanent peace between the states is possible." All the arguments which the philosophes had adduced to show that humanity was approaching a new era of peace seemed fallacious to Hamilton. Commerce had not softened the manners of men and extinguished the lust for war. "Has commerce hitherto done any thing more than change the objects of war? . . . Have there not been as many wars founded upon commercial motives since that has be-

[45] On June 18 and June 29; see *The Records of the Federal Convention of 1787*, vol. i, pp. 297, 307, 466-467.

come the prevailing system of nations, as were before occasioned by the cupidity of territory or dominion?"[46] Nor did Hamilton accept the view that the rise of republicanism could produce a more pacific spirit among nations. "Have republics in practice been less addicted to war than monarchies?" "There have been, if I may so express it, about as many popular as royal wars. The cries of the nation and the importunities of their representatives have, upon various occasions, dragged their monarchs into war, or continued them in it, contrary to their inclination, and sometimes contrary to the real interests of the state." Hamilton concluded his refutation of philosophic utopianism with what might almost be called a peroration: "Have we not already seen enough of the fallacy and extravagance of those idle theories which have amused us with promises of an exemption from the imperfections, weaknesses, and evils incident to society in every shape? Is it not time to awake from the deceitful dream of a golden age, and to adopt as a practical maxim for the direction of our political conduct that we, as well as the other inhabitants of the globe, are yet remote from the happy empire of perfect wisdom and perfect virtue?"

With his refutation of what he believed to be dangerously illusionist views on foreign policy, Hamilton cleared the way for presenting what he considered the right course for American foreign policy. In explaining his positive views, Hamilton showed himself deeply steeped in the ways of thinking of the practical diplomats and of the writers on the interests of the states; he followed them in concepts and methods. Foreign policy is nothing but a striving for greater power; state is opposed to state, neighbors are a country's "natural enemies." Like the writers on the doctrine of the interests of the states, Hamilton found in the functioning of the "balance of power"

[46] No. vi of *The Federalist*; see also nos. vii and xi for the quotations from *The Federalist*.

the one contrivance which could set limits to the power drive of the individual state. According to Hamilton every discussion of foreign policy must start from these assumptions: they provide the basis for determining the political system, within which American foreign policy must work, and for defining America's "true interest."

Hamilton believed—and here again he followed closely the doctrine of the interests of the states—that there were several political systems in the world, each of them linking together those states whose interests touched upon each other. Hamilton distinguished four of them: "The world may politically, as well as geographically, be divided into four parts, each having a distinct set of interests": Europe, Africa, Asia, and America. In distinguishing an American from a European system, Hamilton implied that America should not aim at playing a role in the European balance of power, but withdraw from Europe. America could not dispense with power politics—power competition would also rule in the American sphere—but if she would keep away from the rivalries of the European states, she would be able to make her whole strength felt in the area with which she was most immediately connected; there America could attain a position of hegemony. "Our situation invites and our interests prompt us to aim at an ascendant in the system of American affairs."

It may appear that Hamilton only restated the views with which, in 1776, the colonists had embarked on foreign policy—that America should have nothing to do with Europe. But if the bare conclusion was the same, it had been arrived at in a very different spirit, and it had widely divergent implications. Not the adoption of a "new policy" which would transform the face of the political world, but the fitting of the "old policy" to the American scene—this was the essence of Hamilton's program for American foreign policy.

CHAPTER V

WASHINGTON'S POLITICAL
TESTAMENT:

The Farewell Address

I

WHEN the last year of Washington's second presidential term had come around, there were no doubts in the President's mind that "ease and retirement" were "indispensably necessary"[1] to him. He now had to decide what form the announcement of his retirement should take and what would be the most appropriate moment for it.

Four years earlier, in 1792, Washington had faced a similar situation. He had wanted to return to his beloved Mount Vernon and retire to the life of a gentleman farmer. When he had asked James Madison about the most suitable procedure for carrying out his intention, Madison had advised the President to announce his decision in a valedictory address to be published in the newspapers in September, so that the people would be informed before the balloting for the presidential electors would start. At last, however, Washington had given in to the urgings of all his political friends who had pressed him to stay on until—and this, they said, would happen in a short time—"public opinion, the character of the Govern-

---

[1] Washington to Jay, May 8, 1796, *Washington's Farewell Address*, ed. Victor Hugo Paltsits, New York 1935, p. 239. Since most of the documents which have bearing upon the genesis and history of Washington's Farewell Address are assembled and reprinted in this book, I shall quote from it.

ment, and the course of its administration should be better decided."[2]

The problems besetting Washington's second administration were far different from those of the first; they also differed widely from the political tasks which he and his friends had envisaged when he had decided to remain in office for another term. The most important tasks of Washington's first presidential term had been the establishment of the new federal administration, the decision on a capital for the United States, and, especially, the determination of the course which the young republic should follow in its financial and economic policy. When Washington's friends had urged him to continue in office because he was needed to give "such a tone and firmness to the Government as would secure it against danger,"[3] they were thinking that these domestic issues demanded further consolidation under a steady government. In Washington's second administration, however, foreign policy, which before 1792 had appeared on the American horizon only intermittently, came into the foreground and dominated the political scene. War had come close to America. The war of the German powers against France broadened into a world conflict when, in February 1793, Great Britain, Holland, and Spain joined the struggle against the French Revolution. The British blockade of France impinged on the pursuit of American trade. An attack by England and Spain against the French possessions in the West Indies might lead France to demand American assistance in accordance with the Franco-American alliance of 1778. Yet American involvement in the war was the more dangerous because the colonies of England and Spain on the North American continent encircled the frontiers of the United States; it seemed unlikely that its boundaries could be defended against the joint operations of Britain and Spain. In

[2] *Ibid.*, p. 215.　　　　　　　　[3] *Ibid.*, pp. 215, 216.

the month following his second inauguration, on April 22, 1793, Washington issued a "Proclamation of Neutrality" announcing the decision to "adopt and pursue a conduct friendly and impartial towards the Belligerent Powers." The President advised the citizens of the United States to avoid all acts which might be in contradiction to this attitude and threatened them with loss of protection and, if possible, prosecution in case they should violate the laws of neutrality. Although the Proclamation of Neutrality established the course which America would try to follow throughout the European conflict, the pressure of events made it frequently questionable whether the United States could hold to this position. When the Proclamation was issued, the newly appointed minister of the French Republic, Genêt, had already reached American soil and had begun his attempt to draw the United States into the war—by one-sided interpretation of the articles of the old alliance, by inflammatory appeals to the citizens over the heads of the government, and by directly unneutral acts like the equipping of French privateers in America. Genêt overplayed his hand. In the summer of 1793, Washington's government agreed on the necessity of his recall. Although Genêt's provocative attitude cooled the passionately pro-French sentiments prevalent among wide groups of the American public, this advantage for the advocates of a neutral policy was soon counter-balanced by the irritating attitude of the British government towards America. The actions of the British navy showed a blatant disregard of the American views on the rights of neutrals in wartime. Moreover, from Canada came disquieting news which raised suspicion of a military attack from the north. If gratitude for French assistance in the War of Independence and sympathy for republicanism had not been strong enough to bring the United States into war on the French side, the old hatred against George III, reawakened by the highhandedness of the British government, might provide the spark which would start the fires of war. During the spring of 1794, Washington decided to send John Jay as a special envoy to Britain—an almost desperate attempt by direct negotiations to avoid further aggravation of British-American relations.

It took almost a year, till March 1795, for the results of Jay's negotiations to become known in America. With the exception of one significant concession—the evacuation of the northern frontier posts—the British had not yielded to American wishes. They refused to abandon interference with neutral shipping in wartime. The Jay Treaty was of little avail in changing the minds of those who believed that America's place was on the side of France or that a neutrality benevolent towards France rather than an impartial neutrality was the right course for America. When the Jay Treaty was presented to the Senate for ratification in the summer of 1795, a vehement struggle developed; but the treaty was accepted with a number of votes just equalling the constitutionally necessary two-thirds majority. Washington was able to ratify the treaty.

In the light of later developments, the value of the Jay Treaty for the preservation of a neutral course in American foreign policy must be regarded as doubtful. French resentment over the conclusion of the Jay Treaty resulted in the "undeclared war against France," and the unsolved differences in the British and American views on neutrality played their part in the origin of the Anglo-American War of 1812. But Washington regarded his second term as full of lasting achievements in foreign policy. Through the Proclamation of 1793, he had set the American course towards neutrality. Without dissolving the French alliance, he had refused to interpret it as a restriction on American freedom of action. Finally, he had diminished the danger of conflict between Britain and America by a settlement which, unsatisfactory as it might be in its details, removed the risk of sudden explosion. This was the reason for the optimism with which Washington had greeted Congress at the opening of its session in December 1795: "I have never met you at any period, when more than at present, the situation of our public affairs has afforded just cause for mutual congratulation."[4] It was true that a large percentage of the public remained hostile to the government, but even this cloud was disappearing. Washington believed he could notice that in January and February "a great change has been wrought in the public mind"[5] and that the people were beginning to recognize the merits of his foreign policy.

This was the time when Washington's thoughts turned to the problems involved in announcing his intention to retire. He thought it best, as we can deduce from indications about a conversation with Alexander Hamilton in the second half of February, to use the draft for a valedictory address which Madison had set up in 1792, but to add a further section about the experiences of his second administration.

Events intervened which must have pushed such thoughts into the background. For in March it became clear that the struggle over the Jay Treaty had not ended with its acceptance by the Senate. When the House of Representatives was asked to approve the expenditures necessary for the implementation of the treaty, the Republicans under Madison's leadership tried to upset the whole arrangement by refusing this financial request. The outcome of this great debate was uncertain until the last moment. It is evident that the renewal of the struggle over the Jay Treaty put a new construction on Washington's plans for retirement. If the opponents of the treaty had won out, this would have

[4] Washington, *Writings*, ed. John C. Fitzpatrick, vol. xxxiv, Washington 1940, p. 386.
[5] Washington to Gouverneur Morris, March 4, 1796, *ibid.*, p. 483.

been a rejection of the government; and Washington's unwillingness to stand for another term could have hardly been presented as a voluntary act. It did not come to this; on April 30, 1796, by a vote of 51 to 48, the House approved the funds necessary for the implementation of the treaty.

To Washington, the debate on the Jay Treaty was one of the most important events in the history of the young republic. This was not just because approval or rejection of his foreign policy was involved. Washington viewed the attempt of the House to influence foreign policy by means of its power over the purse as a violation of the Constitution, which had confided the treaty-making power to the President and the Senate. Interference by the House in foreign affairs could be explained only as an invasion of the rights of others and an attempt to enlarge its own power. Washington saw the entire Constitution brought "to the brink of a precipice."[6]

Although the debate in the House over the Jay Treaty in March and April 1796 had shown the strength of partisan divisions in the field of foreign policy, the result was not entirely negative. Positively, the outcome of the debate represented an approval of the foreign policy of the government, and it had also clarified the constitutional issues involved in the conduct of foreign policy. Washington could rightly consider that if his first administration had established the foundations for the internal organization of the republic, his second administration had laid out the course for the management of foreign affairs. In May, Washington was free to turn again to the problems of his valedictory address. He sent his draft of a valedictory address to Alexander Hamilton, on whom he was accustomed to rely for help in the composition of state documents. This draft

[6] Washington to Charles Carroll, May 1, 1796, *ibid.*, vol. xxxv, p. 30.

represented no great change from the ideas which he had expressed in February. In the first part of the draft, Washington reproduced the valedictory address which Madison had prepared for him in 1792. Then there followed a new part which, as Washington wrote to Hamilton, had become necessary because of "considerable changes having taken place both at home and abroad."[7] The addition shows that Washington regarded the events in the field of foreign affairs as the central issues of his second administration.

II

The tone of the part which Washington had written to complement Madison's draft was very different from that of the valedictory of 1792. Taking a stand high above concrete and disputed political issues and expressing generally acceptable sentiments, Madison had woven together a justification of Washington's decision to retire, a praise of the American Constitution, and an exhortation to preserve the advantages of the Union.

In the part which Washington added in 1796, the closeness and the bitterness of the political fights of the preceding months and years were clearly noticeable. The last five paragraphs of this section mentioned the attacks against the government and the abuses to which the President had been subjected. Washington's statement that his "fortune, in a pecuniary point of view, has received no augmentation from my country"[8] showed how he had been hurt by the recent criticisms resulting from revelations according to which he had temporarily overdrawn his accounts with the government. The section which stands between Madison's draft and the last five paragraphs of personal defense, and which forms the most important part of Washington's addition, is

[7] *Washington's Farewell Address*, p. 168.
[8] *Ibid.*, p. 173.

the section in which foreign policy has the most prominent role.

It consists of a number of different, only loosely connected thoughts, moulded in the form of a list of "wishes,"[9] as Washington himself called them. Of these nine wishes, only the first two and the last are not directly concerned with foreign policy. However, the first wish—an admonition to extinguish or, at least, moderate party disputes—and the last—a counsel to maintain the constitutional delimitations of powers—were inspired by developments in the area of foreign policy, by the bitterness of party differences revealed in the debate over the Jay Treaty, and by the attempt of the House to have a part in the making of treaties. The remaining six wishes, which refer to issues of foreign policy, summarized Washington's experiences in his second administration. Essentially, they were ideas which Washington had expressed at other places in the same or similar form. Washington's first three recommendations in the field of foreign affairs—scrupulously to observe treaty obligations, to refrain from political connections, and to take pride in America as a distinct nation—can be found, more briefly but in the same sequence, in a letter from Washington to Patrick Henry in October 1795. In his draft for the valedictory, Washington elaborated on the dangers of foreign interference in American politics and on the necessity of realizing that in foreign affairs, each nation is guided exclusively by egoistic motives. The following wish—that America must do everything possible to keep the peace for twenty years, until which time her position would be almost unassailable—was a revision of a paragraph in a letter from Washington to Gouverneur Morris of December 22, 1795. The last two pieces of advice—the need for maintaining a truly neutral attitude and for preserving the Union as a

[9] *Ibid.*, p. 168.

check against destructive intentions of foreign powers—
Washington had also voiced previously.

The part of Washington's draft dealing with foreign
affairs represents a collection of diverse thoughts and ideas
which are neither closely integrated nor systematically
organized. Yet one theme permeates the various paragraphs:
a warning against the spirit of faction and against the danger
of letting ideological predilections and prejudices enter considerations of foreign policy. This is the topic of the central
paragraph in Washington's list of "wishes," where he
admonished the citizens to take "pride in the name of an
American." The same theme appears in the paragraphs on
the duties of neutrals and the need for union; it is impres-
sively stated as Washington's first "wish," in which he
implored the citizens to use "charity and benevolence"
towards each other in case of political differences and
dissensions.

Washington did not provide an analysis of the international situation into which America had been placed. Nor
did he describe the course which, as a result of such an
analysis, America ought to follow in foreign policy. He
touched upon these points, but only lightly and selectively,
almost accidentally. Washington's fundamental concern was
the attitude of American citizens towards foreign policy and
the need for overcoming party spirit in decisions on foreign
policy.

III

Washington's condemnation of the spirit of faction arose
from a deep political conviction. Although differences in
political opinions might be unavoidable, Washington believed that rational discussion would always lead to a
realization of the true interest of the nation. Washington
saw himself standing above the parties, forcing the conten-

tious politicians to work together under the uniting banner of the true national interest. He had tried to keep Jefferson and Hamilton in the government even when their political differences had nearly paralyzed the functioning of the administration.

In 1796, it was an equally strange idea to bring Hamilton and Madison together in a common task. One cannot help wondering whether, in giving both Hamilton and Madison a part in the composition of his valedictory, Washington might have hoped that he could make this document a further demonstration of his conviction that party contrasts did not exclude cooperation in a situation of national interest and that this cooperation would lend added weight to his valedictory pronouncement, securing it against the objection of being an expression of personal or partisan views.

During the preceding years, Hamilton and Madison had emerged as the leaders of the two opposing parties, the Federalists and the Republicans. Both parties maintained that their differences were irreconcilable, because each believed the other was trying to overthrow the Constitution. To the Republicans, Washington had become an enemy, a prisoner of the Federalists. On the other hand, the Federalists, who characterized Madison as an irresponsible radical, could not look approvingly upon the possible increase in Madison's reputation resulting from his collaboration in Washington's valedictory.

When, in February 1796, Washington had told Hamilton of his plan of issuing a valedictory which would consist of two parts, the one which Madison had drafted in 1792 and the other an addition for which he asked Hamilton's assistance, Hamilton expressed his reservations immediately. Hamilton preferred an entirely new document; he seems also to have raised special objections to the contents of

Madison's draft and to the mention of Madison's name in the valedictory.

But Washington stuck to his plan. On May 12, 1796, Washington invited Madison to dinner, probably to talk with him about his retirement. Washington might have thought he could hardly use Madison's draft for a valedictory, still less in a changed form, without informing him. Although Madison might have felt little enthusiasm for collaborating with Washington at a time when he was sharply opposed to the President's policy, he certainly had no valid reason for objecting. The valedictory of 1792 had been written in close adherence to Washington's instructions and placed at Washington's disposal.

Three days later, on May 15, 1796, Washington sent to Hamilton material for revision which consisted of a brief introduction, Madison's draft, and the lengthy addition necessitated by the "considerable changes having taken place both at home and abroad." Washington had made a concession to Hamilton's views by omitting, contrary to his original intention, a direct mention of Madison's name and by leaving out a few passages from Madison's draft. Moreover, the President permitted Hamilton "to throw the whole into a different form."[10] But as Washington indicated, he preferred his original idea of a valedictory address which contained the draft of 1792 and his recently composed additions. Even if Hamilton should decide to give the valedictory an entirely new form, he should submit at the same time another draft which would be restricted to emendations and corrections of the papers Washington had sent him.

After the debate on the Jay Treaty in the House, which had increased party bitterness, Hamilton must have found the idea of Madison's associating with Washington in the

[10] *Ibid.*, p. 241.

announcement of the President's retirement more inappropriate than ever. Moreover, the high praise of Republican government contained in Madison's draft could be interpreted as favoring an attitude to which Hamilton was violently opposed, that of placing America on the side of the French Revolution.

Thus Hamilton was anxious to dissuade Washington from letting the valedictory appear in the form Washington intended. Hamilton could hardly leave this to chance; thus he deliberately employed a method which promised a politically successful outcome. Instead of starting his work by amending and correcting the material which Washington had sent him, he first wrote an entirely new draft, making free use of Washington's permission to "throw the whole into a different form." On July 30, Hamilton was able to send this new draft to Washington with an accompanying letter in which he said that he was now beginning with his work on the second part of Washington's request, namely, with the corrections and improvements of the papers which Washington had sent him in May. However, he added immediately that "I confess the more I have considered the matter the less eligible this plan has appeared to me. There seems to be a certain awkwardness in the thing . . . . Besides that, I think that there are some ideas which will not wear well in the former address . . . ."[11] The presentation of an entirely new and carefully worked out draft, combined with deprecatory remarks about Washington's original plan, did its work. When, on August 10, Hamilton sent to Washington a "draft for incorporating," as Hamilton called his revision of the material which Washington had sent him in May, Washington had become accustomed to the idea of using Hamilton's "Original Major Draft" for his valedictory address.

[11] *Ibid.*, p. 249.

IV

Hamilton was at work on the "Original Major Draft" for Washington's valedictory from the second part of May till far into July. Hamilton's wife, in her old age, still remembered that "the address was written, principally at such times as his Office was seldom frequented by his clients and visitors, and during the absence of his students to avoid interruption; at which times he was in the habit of calling me to sit with him, that he might read to me as he wrote, in order, as he said, to discover how it sounded upon the ear, and making the remark, 'My dear Eliza, you must be to me what Molière's old nurse was to him.' "[12] The care and deliberateness with which Hamilton proceeded suggests that he was impressed by the importance as well as by the difficulty of the task.

Among the considerations which influenced Hamilton in the composition of the document, his eagerness to avoid inserting Madison's valedictory of 1792 was only one, and probably not the most important one. Despite the attacks against Washington in the last years of his second term, the President enjoyed still greater authority and reputation than any other American political leader; the thoughts which he would express when he announced his final retirement from office were bound to make a deep impact on American political thinking. Hamilton must have been well aware that participation in the drafting of Washington's valedictory gave him a unique opportunity to impress on the minds of Americans some of his favorite political ideas. But he was certainly not guided exclusively by personal ambition and party interest. For almost twenty years, Hamilton had been Washington's close collaborator, and he must have felt a

[12] Allan McLane Hamilton, *The Intimate Life of Alexander Hamilton*, New York 1910, p. 111.

selfless obligation to give a dignified form to the final political manifesto of the man whom he had served and admired. Yet Hamilton's work was made still more difficult because he knew that although Washington had little confidence in his own literary gifts, he was a man of "strong penetration" and "sound judgment."[13] Washington would not place his name under a document which he could not regard as an expression of his own mind and ideas.

Thus Hamilton's draft, although very different from the material which Washington had sent him, embodied in form and substance much of Washington's draft. A paper has been preserved which permits an insight into Hamilton's working methods: an "abstract of points to form an address."[14] It lists 23 points containing brief statements of the issues with which he wanted to deal, presenting them more or less in the sequence of the Farewell Address. Of these 23 points, 13 are brief excerpts or paraphrases of Washington's draft. In the middle, from the 10th to the 19th point, Hamilton abandoned close adherence to Washington's draft, enlarging Washington's ideas and adducing new material. Thus the list of points reveals that although Hamilton did not accept Washington's plan of inserting Madison's draft of 1792 as a whole, he had few objections to the ideas outlined by Madison and Washington; indeed, he was willing to incorporate them almost literally. However, he felt the document should be strengthened; it ought to receive more body and substance.

This view is confirmed by the form which Hamilton's draft finally took. The first eight paragraphs, announcing Washington's intention to retire from political life and expressing his wishes for the future prosperity of America

[13] Jefferson on Washington, quoted in John Alexander Carroll and Mary Wells Ashworth (completing the Biography of Douglas Southall Freeman), *George Washington*, vol. vii, New York 1957, p. 653.

[14] *Washington's Farewell Address*, pp. 174-178.

under a free constitution, are closely modeled after Washington's draft. Then Hamilton let Washington say, "Here perhaps I ought to stop." But he did not do so, because solicitude for the welfare of the American people urged him "to offer some sentiments the result of mature reflection confirmed by observation and experience which appear to me essential to the permanency of your felicity as a people"; these sentiments should be received as "the disinterested advice of a parting friend."[15]

With these sentences Hamilton launched a discussion leading far beyond the thoughts contained in Washington's draft. From the point of view of contents as well as from the point of view of length, this section gave the Farewell Address its real weight.

After this, Hamilton returned to a phraseology startlingly similar to that which he had used in introducing the section; he said that "in offering to you, my countrymen, these counsels of an old and affectionate friend—counsels suggested by laborious reflection, and matured by a various experience, I dare not hope that they will make the strong and lasting impressions I wish. . . ."[16] Then there followed six paragraphs of personal justification, which in contents and phraseology were patterned after the end of Washington's draft.

Thus Hamilton's chief contribution to Washington's Farewell Address was the central section of the document, which replaced the "list of wishes" of Washington's draft. Nevertheless, the theme of Washington's list of wishes, the warning against partisanship in foreign policy, was fully expressed; however, it was set in the wider framework of a general survey of domestic and foreign policy.

Hamilton gave the greatest attention to the section on

[15] *Ibid.*, p. 182.
[16] *Ibid.*, p. 198. See also the Appendix for this and the following analyses.

foreign policy. Whereas the reflections on domestic policy corresponded to the outline given in his "abstract of points," the statement on foreign policy was entirely remodeled.

The transition from domestic policy to foreign policy followed smoothly from a warning against party spirit which opens the door to intrigues by foreigners and may lead to attachments in which the smaller nation will revolve around the larger one "as its satellite."

At this point, Hamilton repeated Washington's advice to "avoid connecting ourselves with the politics of any Nation." Hamilton was somewhat more cautious than Washington. He recommended having "as little political connection . . . as possible." Departing from Washington's draft, Hamilton did not say anything at this point about commercial relations but rather went on to justify the advice to abstain from political connections.

The necessity for this attitude, Hamilton believed, followed from the natural situation of things. Each state has certain fundamental interests which it must follow in its policy. If states are in close proximity to each other, their interests touch upon each other and clashes are unavoidable. If America were to ally herself with one of the European powers, she would inevitably have to participate in every European conflict. Such a connection with European power politics would be "artificial"; America was so distant from Europe that she did not belong "naturally" to the European system. From this analysis, Hamilton deduced a "general principle of policy" for America. Although in particular emergencies America might be forced to make a temporary alliance, permanent alliances must be avoided. In its practical consequences, this was not very different from what Washington had said in his draft. But Washington had stressed the weakness of the United States which, within the next twenty years, would make involvement in a war extremely dangerous for the existence of the young republic. By removing the time limit from this piece of advice, by basing it on unchangeable geographical conditions, and by presenting it as a principle of policy, Hamilton made the recommendation in his draft weightier, more impressive, and more apodictic.

It is significant that Hamilton treated with commerce after he had discussed the question of alliances. To him, regulation of commercial relations remained subordinated to power politics. Although America's aim should be the widest possible liberalization of commerce, a certain flexibility in practice was necessary. Commerce was a weapon in the struggle of power politics; in the arrangement of their commercial relations, nations did not follow idealistic principles but only their interests. With the exhortation to recognize national egoism as the driving force in international relations, Hamilton concluded the "counsels of an old and affectionate friend."

In its terminology and formulations, the section on foreign policy echoed expressions and thoughts which had dominated the discussion of foreign affairs ever since America had entered the scene of foreign policy in 1776. We are reminded of Paine's *Common Sense*. We find the word "entangle" which in America had developed into a technical term for characterizing the dangerous consequences of involvement in European politics. We see the distinction between "artificial" and "natural" connections, reflecting the Enlightenment belief in a progress from a world of power politics to an era of permanent peace and increasing prosperity. We recall the famous resolution of Congress of 1783 that "the true interest of these states requires that they should be as little as possible entangled in the politics and controversies of European nations."

This use, in the Farewell Address, of terms and concepts

which had been continuously applied in the discussion of foreign affairs might have been intentional. Hamilton might have felt that these reflections would be more acceptable if they appeared as a restatement of currently held views rather than as a presentation of new ideas. But behind this façade of customary terms and concepts, there was a structure of thought which was Hamilton's own.

Whether Hamilton drafted this part of the Farewell Address with the help of documents which he had previously written, or whether the similarities to his previous works on foreign policy came from such firm and definite convictions that they always took the same expression, we cannot know. In any case, just a year before Hamilton began to work on the Farewell Address, he wrote under the name Horatius a defense of the Jay Treaty which contained a warning against entanglement "in all the contests, broils and wars of Europe" in words very similar to those used in the Farewell Address.[17] Some of the formulations which the Farewell Address and the Horatius paper have in common can also be found in the Memorandum of September 15, 1790, the first written presentation of Hamilton's opinions on foreign affairs as a member of Washington's Cabinet. In this search for ancestors of the Farewell Address among Hamilton's previous writings, we might go back still further to the *Federalist*.

There are passages in Hamilton's draft of the Farewell Address which correspond closely to ideas in the *Federalist*, making it almost certain that Hamilton had this book not only on his bookshelf—as would have been a matter of course—but also on his writing desk when he drafted the Farewell Address. The warning in the Address against wars resulting from the passions of people was a restatement of

[17] Alexander Hamilton, *Works*, ed. Henry Cabot Lodge, vol. v, New York 1904, pp. 181-185.

Hamilton's argument in the sixth number of the *Federalist*, that "there have been . . . almost as many popular as royal wars." Stylistic similarities also exist between the eleventh number of the *Federalist* and passages of the Farewell Address on foreign policy. Ideas which in the Address were only vaguely adumbrated were more clearly expressed in the eleventh number of the *Federalist*. In the Farewell Address, emphasis was laid on Europe's possessing a special political system; the consequence of this point—that America had a political system of her own—was only suggested. The statement in the eleventh number of the *Federalist* that the United States ought "to aim at an ascendant in the system of American affairs" revealed Hamilton's full thought. Because Washington hardly would have liked this open announcement of an aggressive imperialist program, Hamilton refrained from expressing this idea explicitly in the Farewell Address.

The relationship between the Farewell Address and the *Federalist* is particularly important because it shows that although Hamilton used Washington's ideas and statements of others, he placed them in a different setting and gave them a new meaning.

The law of action propounded by Hamilton in the Farewell Address was presented as the specific application of general laws ruling in the political world. It was derived from the geographical division of the earth and from the principle which dominated the life of every state: striving to increase power in line with its fundamental interests. States situated in the same geographical area were tied together in a continuous power struggle arising from clashing interests. They were members of the same political system which extended as far as its natural geographical limits. In Hamilton's formulation, the warning against connection with European power politics was derived neither from a fear of strengthening the centrifugal forces in American political life, as it dominated Washington's thoughts, nor from utopian hopes in an imminent end of the era of power politics and national division, as the founders of American independence had hoped. To Hamilton, sovereign states, competition among them, and power politics were necessary factors in social life; successful political action depended on proceeding according to these presuppositions. Hamilton presented his advice as the necessary consequence of political science; he conceived it as an application of the eternal laws of politics to the American situation. The separation of America from Europe's foreign policy was desirable not because it might be the beginning of a change, of a reform of diplomacy, but because it corresponded to what the political writers had discovered about the political practice of the time. The intellectual framework of the recommendations on foreign policy in the Farewell Address was that of the school of the interests of the state. This is reflected not only in the phraseology and the argumentation, but also in Hamilton's attempt to summarize these counsels in a "great rule of conduct," a "general principle."

When Hamilton sent his draft to Washington, he wrote that he had tried "to render this act importantly and lastingly useful."[18] We can now better understand what these words meant. Hamilton wanted Washington to leave to his successors an explanation of the principles which had guided his policy, just as other rulers and statesmen of the eighteenth century were accustomed to doing in their Political Testaments. In revising Washington's draft for a valedictory, Hamilton transformed it into a Political Testament.

[18] *Washington's Farewell Address*, p. 249.

V

The "great rule" which Washington had set down in the Farewell Address served as a guide to American foreign policy for over a century; of all the Political Testaments of the eighteenth century, the Farewell Address alone succeeded in achieving practical political significance.

Some part of its influence is due to the "accidents of politics," to events in which the United States had, at best, a supporting role. The conflicts of the Napoleonic era and the weakening of the Spanish power broke the ring which foreign colonial possessions had laid around the territory of the United States. As long as several European states were close neighbors, the advice to avoid alliances was an ideal to be pursued rather than a feasible proposition. It became a workable policy only when effective rule by a foreign power was restricted to the north of the continent. The political separation of America from the European power struggle was strengthened by changes which took place in Europe. Nationalism and industrialism shifted the interests of the European powers, and the competition among them, into new channels. Thus, in the nineteenth century, conditions came into existence under which America's foreign policy could become a policy of isolation.

Nevertheless, the profound impact of Washington's counsels in the Farewell Address was also created by features inherent in the document itself. It was the first statement, comprehensive and authoritative at the same time, of the principles of American foreign policy. Hamilton based the discussion of foreign affairs in the Farewell Address on a realistic evaluation of America's situation and interests. Because Hamilton was opposed to American involvement in a war, to which the emotional attachment with France might lead, he emphasized the necessity of neutrality and peace.

The Farewell Address, therefore, could repeat and absorb those views and concepts which expressed the mood of a more idealistic approach to foreign policy. These elements were not like ghost cities left abandoned outside the main stream of development; they were necessary stations on the road "to the Farewell Address."

Political Testaments, in general, remained closely tied to the eighteenth-century concept of power politics. The integration of idealistic assumptions constitutes the distinguishing feature of the Farewell Address. Thus it could have an appeal in the following century of rising democracy when foreign policy demanded legitimation by clearly felt and recognized values and needed to be conducted in accordance with the will of the people.

Because the Farewell Address comprises various aspects of American political thinking, it reaches beyond any period limited in time and reveals the basic issue of the American attitude toward foreign policy: the tension between Idealism and Realism. Settled by men who looked for gain and by men who sought freedom, born into independence in a century of enlightened thinking and of power politics, America has wavered in her foreign policy between Idealism and Realism, and her great historical moments have occurred when both were combined. Thus the history of the Farewell Address forms only part of a wider, endless, urgent problem. This study is an attempt to shed light on its beginnings. With the analysis of the diverse intellectual trends which went into the making of the Farewell Address, with the description of its genesis, our story ends.

Appendix

In ORDER to clarify the discussion in Chapter V, the sections concerned with foreign policy, both in the final text of the Farewell Address and in its various drafts, are printed below. The documents are reproduced in the form in which they have been published by Victor Hugo Paltsits, *Washington's Farewell Address*, New York 1935, but Paltsits' work indicates corrections, deletions, passages written in the margin, etc.; these details have been left out here.

A. *Washington's First Draft for an Address*

Enclosed in his letter of May 15, 1796 to Hamilton

[After Washington had presented the draft which Madison had made for him in 1792, he added:]

Had the situation of our public affairs continued to wear the same aspect they assumed at the time the aforegoing address was drawn I should not have taken the liberty of troubling you—my fellow citizens—with any new sentiments or with a repition [sic for repetition], more in detail, of those which are therein contained; but considerable changes having taken place both at home and abroad, I shall ask your indulgence while I express with more lively sensibility, the following most ardent wishes of my heart[.]

That party disputes, among all the friends and lovers of their country may subside, or, as the wisdom of Providence hath ordained that men, on the same subjects, shall not always think alike, that charity and benevolence when they happen to differ may so far shed their benign influence as to banish those invectives which proceed from illiberal prejudices and jealousy.—

That as the allwise dispensor of human blessings has favored no Nation of the Earth with more abundant, and substantial means of happiness than United America, that we may not be so ungrateful to our Creator—so wanting to

[137]

ourselves—and so regardless of Posterity—as to dash the cup of beneficence which is thus bountifully offered to our acceptance.

That we may fulfil with the greatest exactitude *all* our engagements: foreign and domestic, to the *utmost* of our abilities whensoever, and in whatsoever manner they are pledged: for in public, as in private life, I am persuaded that honesty will forever be found to be the best policy[.]

That we may avoid connecting ourselves with the Politics of any Nation, farther than shall be found necessary to regulate our own trade; in order that commerce may be placed upon a stable footing—our merchants know their rights—and the government the ground on which those rights are to be supported.—

That every citizen would take pride in the name of an American, and act as if he felt the importance of the character by considering that we ourselves are now a distinct Nation the dignity of which will be absorbed, if not annihilated, if we enlist ourselves (further than our obligations may require) under the banners of any other Nation whatsoever.—And moreover, that we would guard against the Intriegues of *any* and *every* foreign Nation who shall endeavor to intermingle (however covertly and indirectly) in the internal concerns of our country—or who shall attempt to prescribe rules for our policy with any other power, if their be no infraction of our engagements with themselves, as one of the greatest evils that can befal us as a people; for whatever may be their professions, be assured fellow Citizens and the event will (as it always has) invariably prove, that Nations as well as individuals, act for their own benefit, and not for the benefit of others, unless both interests happen to be assimilated (and when that is the case there requires no contract to bind them together)—That all their interferences are calculated to promote the former; and in proportion as they succeed, will render us less independant.—In a word, nothing is more certain than that, if we receive favors, we must grant favors; and it is not easy to decide beforehand under such circumstances as we are, on which side the balance will ultimately terminate—but easy indeed is it to foresee that it may involve us in disputes and finally in War, to fulfil political alliances.—Whereas, if there be no engagements on our part, we shall be unembarrassed, and at liberty at all times, to act from circumstances, and the dictates of Justice—sound policy—and our essential Interests.—

That we may be always prepared for War, but never unsheath the sword except in self defence so long as Justice and our *essential* rights, and national respectibility can be preserved without it—for without the spirit of divination, it may safely be pronounced, that if this country can remain in peace 20 years longer—and I devoutly pray that it may do so to the end of time—such in all probability will be its population, riches and resources, when combined with its peculiarly happy and remote Situation from the other quarters of the globe—as to bid defiance, in a just cause, to any earthly power whatsoever.—

That whensoever, and so long as we profess to be Neutral, let our public conduct whatever our private affections may be, accord therewith; without suffering partialities on one hand, or prejudices on the other to controul our Actions.— A contrary practice is not only incompatible with our declarations, but is pregnant with mischief—embarrassing to the Administration—tending to divide us into parties— and ultimately productive of all those evils and horrors which proceed from faction—and above all.

That our Union may be lasting as time.—for While we are encircled in one band we shall possess the strength of a Giant and there will be none who can make us affraid— Divide, and we shall become weak; a prey to foreign Intriegues and internal discord:—and shall be as miserable and contemptible as we are now enviable and happy——— And lastly—

That the several departments of Government may be preserved in their utmost Constitutional purity, without any attempt of the one to encroach on the rights or priviledges of another—that the Genl and State governm^ts may move in their prop^r Orbits—And that the authorities of our own constituting may be respected by ourselves as the most certain means of having them respected by foreigners.—In expressing these sentiments it will readily be perceived that I can have no view now—whatever malevolence might have ascribed to it before—than such as result from a perfect conviction of the utility of the measure.—If public servants, in the exercise of their official duties are found incompetent or pursuing wrong courses discontinue them.—If they are guilty of mal-practices in office, let them be more ex[em]plarily punished—in both cases the Constitution and Laws have made provision, but do not withdraw your confidence from them—the best incentive to a faithful discharge of their duty—without just cause; nor infer, because measures of a complicated nature—which, time, opportunity and close investigation alone can penetrate, and for these reasons are not easily comprehended by those who do not possess the means, that it necessarily follows they must be wrong;—This would not only be doing injustice to your Trustees, but be counteracting your own essential interests —rendering those Trustees (if not contemptable in the eyes of the world) little better at least than cyphers in the Administration of the government and the Constitution of your own chusing would reproach you for such conduct.

[Washington continued with three paragraphs defending the record of his administration.]

B. *Hamilton's Abstract of Points to form an Address*
Undated, but before July 5, 1796

[The "points" referring to foreign affairs are the following:]

XIV   Cherish Good Faith Justice and Peace with other Nations—
1. Because Religion and morality dictate it
2. Because Policy dictates it

If there could exist a nation invariably honest and fait[h]ful the benefits would be immense

But avoid national antipathies or national attachments *display the Evils*—fertil source of Wars—instrument of *ambitious Rulers*

XV Republics peculiarly exposed to foreign intrigue those sentiments lay them open to it.

XVI. The greater rule of our foreign politics ought to be to have as little political connections as possible with foreign Nations

establishing temporary & convenient rules that commerce may be placed on a stable footing Merchants know their rights & Commerce how to support them —not seeking *favors*

Cultivating Commerce with all by gentle & natural means diffusing & diversyfying it but *forcing nothing* —& Cherish the sentiment of *independence* taking pride in the appellation of Amer[i]ca

XVII—Our seperation from Europe renders standing alliances inexpedient—subjecting our peace & interest to the primary to the primary [sic] & complicated relations of European interests—

Keeping constantly in view to place ourselves upon a respectable *defensive* and if forced into Controversy trusting to Connections of the Occasion—

XVIII Our Attitude imposing and rendering this policy safe

But this must be with the exception of existing engagements to be preserved but not extended—

XIX It is not expected that these admonitions can controul the course of the human passions but if they only moderate them in some instances and now and then excite the reflections of virtue [in] men heated by party spirit my endeavor is rewarded

XX How far in the administration of my present Office my conduct has conformed to these principle[s] records must witness—My conscience assures me that I believed myself to be guided by them—

XXI Particularly in relation to the Present War. The Proclamation of the 22 of April 1793 is the key to my plan— Approved [by] your Voice and that of your Representatives in Congress the spirit of that measure

Touch sentiments with regard to conduct of belligerent Powers a wish that France may establish good Government—

Time everything.

has continually guided me uninfluenced by&regardless of the Complaints&attempts of any [of] the powers at war or their partizans to change them—

I thought our Country had a right under all the circumstances to take this ground and I was resolved as far as depended on me to maintain it firmly—

C. *Hamilton's Original Major Draft for an Address called "Copy considerably amended"*

This draft is undated but was sent by Hamilton to Washington on July 30, 1796.

[The section concerned with foreign policy and reproduced below forms less than one-eighth of the full text.]

Excessive partiality for one foreign nation and excessive dislike of another, leads to see danger only on one side and serves to viel [sic for veil] and second the arts of influence on the other - - - Real Patriots who resist the intrigues of the favorite become suspected and odious—Its tools and dupes usurp the applause and confidence of the people to betray their interests—

The great rule of conduct for us in regard to foreign Nations ought to be to have as little *political* connection with them as possible—So far as we have already formed engagements let them be fulfilled—with circumspection indeed but with perfect good faith. Here let us stop—

Europe has a set of primary interests which have none or a very remote relation to us—Hence she must be involved in frequent contests the causes of which will be essentially foreign to us - - - - Hence therefore it must necessarily be unwise on our part to implicate ourselves by an artificial connection in the ordinary vicissitudes of European politics —in the combination, and collisions of her friendships or enmities—

Our detached and distant situation invites us to a different course and enables us to pursue it—If we remain a united people under an efficient Government the period is not distant when we may defy material injury from external annoyance—when we may take such an attitude as will cause the neutrality we shall at any time resolve to observe to be violated with caution—when it will be the interest of belligerent nations under the impossibility of making acquisitions upon us to be very careful how either forced us to throw our weight into the opposite scale—when we may choose peace or war as our interest guided by justice shall dictate.

Why should we forego the advantages of so felicitous a situation? Why quit our own ground to stand upon Foreign ground? Why by interweavi[n]g our destiny with any part of Europe should we intangle our prosperity and peace in the nets of European Ambition rivalship interest or Caprice?

Permanent alliance, intimate connection with any part of the foreign world is to be avoided- - - so far (I mean) as we are now at liberty to do it:- - - for let me never be understood as patronising infidelity to pre-existing engagements—These must be observed in their true and genuine sense—But tis not necessary nor will it be prudent to extend them—'Tis our true policy as a general principle to avoid permanent or close alliance[s]—Taking care always to keep ourselves by suitable establishments in a respectably defensive posture we may safely trust to occasional alliances for extraordinary emergencies.

Harmony liberal intercourse and commerce with all nations—are recommended by justice humanity and interest— But even our commercial policy should hold an equal hand neither seeking nor granting exclusive favours or preferences

—consulting the natural course of things—*diffusing* and *diversifying* by gentle means the streams of Commerce but forcing nothing—establishing with powers so disposed in order to give to Trade a stable course, to define the rights of our Merchants, and enable the Government to support them —conventional rules of intercourse the best that present circumstances and mutual opinion of interest will permit but temporary—and liable to be abandoned [sic] or varied as time experience and future circumstances may dictate—remembering alway that tis folly in one nation to expect disinterested favour in another—that to accept any thing under that character is to part with a portion of its independence— and that it may—find itself in the condition of having given equivalents for nominal favours and of being reproached with ingratitude in the bargain. There can be no greater error in national policy than to desire expect or calculate upon real favours—Tis an illusion that experience must cure, that a just pride ought to discard- - - -

In offering to you My Countrymen! these counsels of an old and affectionate friend—counsels suggested by laborious reflection and matured by a various experience - - - I dare not hope that they will make the strong and lasting impressions I wish—that they will controul the current of the passions or prevent our nation from running the course which has hitherto marked the destiny of all nations—But I may flatter myself that if they even produce some partial benefit, some occasional good- - - that they sometimes recur to moderate the violence of party spirit - - - to warn against the evils of foreign intrigue - - - to guard against the impositions of pretended patriotism - - - the having offered them must always afford me a precious consolation—

D. *Washington's Final Manuscript of the Farewell Address*
Dated September 19, 1796

Excessive partiality for one foreign nation and excessive dislike of another, cause those whom they actuate to see danger only on one side, and serve to veil and even second the arts of influence on the other.—Real Patriots, who may resist the intriegues of the favourite, are liable to become suspected and odious; while its tools and dupes usurp the applause and confidence of the people, to surrender their interests.—

The Great rule of conduct for us, in regard to foreign Nations is in extending our commercial relations to have with them as little *political* connection as possible.—So far as we have already formed engagements let them be fulfilled, with perfect good faith.—Here let us stop.

Europe has a set of primary interests, which to us have none, or a very remote relation.—Hence she must be engaged in frequent controversies, the causes of which are essentially foreign to our concerns.—Hence therefore it must be unwise in us to implicate ourselves, by artificial ties, in the ordinary vicissitudes of her politics, or the ordinary combinations and collisions of her friendships, or enmities:—

Our detached and distant situation invites and enables us to pursue a different course.—If we remain one People, under an efficient government, the period is not far off, when we may defy material injury from external annoyance;— when we may take such an attitude as will cause the neutrality we may at any time resolve upon to be scrupulously respected;—when belligerent nations, under the impossibility of making acquisitions upon us, will not lightly hazard the giving us provocation;—when we may choose peace or war, as our interest guided by justice shall counsel.—

Why forego the advantages of so peculiar a situation?— Why quit our own to stand upon foreign ground?—Why, by interweaving our destiny with that of any part of Europe, entangle our peace and prosperity in the toils of European ambition, Rivalship, Interest, Humour or Caprice?—

'Tis our true policy to steer clear of permanent alliances, with any portion of the foreign world—so far, I mean, as we are now at liberty to do it—for let me not be understood as capable of patronising infidility to existing engagements, (I hold the maxim no less applicable to public than to private affairs, that honesty is always the best policy)—I repeat it therefore, let those engagements be observed in their genuine sense.—But in my opinion, it is unnecessary and would be unwise to extend them.—

Taking care always to keep ourselves, by suitable establishments, on a respectably defensive posture, we may safely trust to temporary alliances for extraordinary emergencies.—

Harmony, liberal intercourse with all nations, are recommended by policy, humanity and interest.—But even our commercial policy should hold an equal and impartial hand:— neither seeking nor granting exclusive favours or preferences;—consulting the natural course of things;— diffusing and deversifying by gentle means the streams of commerce, but forcing nothing;—establishing with Powers so disposed—in order to give to trade a stable course, to define the rights of our merchants, and to enable the Government to support them—conventional rules of intercourse; the best that present circumstances and mutual opinion will permit, but temporary, and liable to be from time to time abandoned or varied, as experience and circumstances shall dictate; constantly keeping in view that 'tis folly in one nation to look for disinterested favors from another—that it must pay with a portion of its Independence for whatever it may accept under that character—that by such acceptance, it may place itself in the condition of having given equivalents for nominal favours and yet of being reproached with ingratitude for not giving more.—There can be no greater error than to expect, or calculate upon real favours from Nation to Nation.—'Tis an illusion which experience must cure, which a just pride ought to discard.—

In offering to you, my Countrymen, these counsels of an old and affectionate friend, I dare not hope they will make the strong and lasting impression, I could wish—that they will controul the usual current of the passions, or prevent our

Nation from running the course which has hitherto marked the Destiny of Nations:—But if I may even flatter myself, that they may be productive of some partial benefit, some occasional good;—that they may now and then recur to moderate the fury of party spirit, to warn against the mischiefs of foreign Intriegue, to guard against the Impostures of pretended patriotism—this hope will be a full recompence for the solicitude for your welfare, by which they have been dictated.

Bibliographical Essay

THE footnotes at the foot of the page throughout the text indicate the sources from which quotations were taken. In the following, the scholarly literature used in the composition of this book will be discussed.

The variety of political events and intellectual trends touched upon in this book made it impossible to list all the books which were used. For a detailed bibliography the reader must refer to the well-known bibliographical guides available for American history and for the history of the European nations.

The following bibliographical essay is limited to those books which, for facts or interpretation, I found particularly useful or suggestive, and this essay will give reasons for statements which are new, or divergent from those of other authors; the passages in the text to which such explanatory remarks belong are indicated by page numbers enclosed in brackets.

CHAPTER I: THE COLONIES AND EUROPE

The problem of the colonial background of American foreign policy is still in need of systematic investigation and comprehensive treatment. The problem has been analyzed only in a number of articles dealing with special aspects of the questions involved. Among such articles I mention three of Max Savelle, "Colonial Origins of American Diplomatic Principles," *Pacific Historical Review*, vol. III (1934), pp. 334-350; "The American Balance of Power and European Diplomacy 1713-78" in *The Era of the American Revolution. Studies inscribed to E. B. Greene*, ed. Richard B. Morris, New York 1939, pp. 140-169, which deals with the repercussions of European diplomacy on the American continent; and

"The Appearance of an American Attitude toward External Affairs, 1750-1775," *American Historical Review*, vol. LII (1947), pp. 655-666. See also Clarence E. Carter, "The Office of Commander in Chief. A Phase of Imperial Unity on the Eve of the Revolution," in *The Era of the American Revolution*, pp. 170-213, and the recent article by John A. Schutz, "Imperialism in Massachusetts during the Governorship of William Shirley, 1741-1756," *The Huntington Library Quarterly*, vol. XXIII (1960), pp. 217-236, which studies the connection between the wars in Europe and the military actions on the North American continent.

Because of the lack of a comprehensive work on the colonial background of American foreign policy, the outline of this problem given in this book is based on material provided by the general works on the political, intellectual, and social history of the colonial period. Throughout the entire chapter I am obligated to Curtis P. Nettels, *The Roots of American Civilization*, New York 1938.

For a recent treatment of the English explorers and the motives which inspired their voyages [p. 4], see A. L. Rowse, *The Elizabethans and America*, New York 1959. The identification of the book, which Sir Humfrey Gilbert was reading on the *Squirrel* as Sir Thomas More's *Utopia* [p. 3] has been frequently made; see, for instance, S. E. Morison and H. S. Commager, *The Growth of the American Republic*, vol. I, New York 1942, p. 35.

The political and administrative developments in the colonies in the seventeenth century are authoritatively described in the classical work by C. M. Andrews, *The Colonial Period of American History*, 4 vols., New Haven 1934-38, of which I have made extensive use, particularly of vol. IV. Perry Miller, *The New England Mind: The Seventeenth Century*, New York 1939, was suggestive for the description of the basic attitude to foreign policy in the northern colonies. Bernard Bailyn, *The New England Merchants in the Seventeenth Century*, Cambridge 1955, sheds light on the changing attitude of the different generations in New England [p. 5].

In comparison to the many recent studies dealing with life in the North American colonies in the seventeenth century, the developments in the colonies in the first half of the eighteenth century have been somewhat neglected, as has been frequently pointed out, see Frederick B. Tolles, "New Approaches to Research in Early American History," *William and Mary Quarterly*, Third Series, vol. xii (1955), pp. 456-461.

Carl Bridenbaugh, *Cities in the Wilderness*, New York 1938, illustrates the changes in social life which stimulated new intellectual activities. Of the works dealing with the early years of Benjamin Franklin, from which much can be gleaned about the intellectual setting of the period, I mention here Gerald Stourzh, *Benjamin Franklin and American Foreign Policy*, Chicago 1954, which places Franklin's ideas in the framework of the European thought of his time. Verner W. Crane, *The Southern Frontier, 1670-1732*, Durham 1928, contains important material on the question of American Union versus colonial autonomy. Crane refers briefly to a report of 1719 by the Governor of Pennsylvania Keith to the Board of Trade. The report which I read in extenso in the Public Record Office is particularly interesting on the question of the contrast between the urgings of the officials of the London Board of Trade towards greater cooperation among the colonies, and the colonists' insistence on colonial autonomy [p. 11]: Keith proposed closer cooperation among the colonies along the lines which the Report of the Board of Trade would suggest in 1720, but Keith did "not expect that his Project will generally please"; he was very much aware of the rivalries between the colonies which make "the traders of New York jealous and uneasie at the proffits gained by the traders of Virginia" and "those again of the Improvements which may possibly be made in Carolina." Keith's report was based on "material" which James Logan had provided, see Frederick B. Tolles, *James Logan and the Culture of Provincial America*, Boston 1957, p. 109, and the publication of Logan's "materials" in Hazard's *Register of Pennsylvania*, vol. III, Philadelphia 1829, pp. 210-212. Logan certainly was representative of an imperialist viewpoint among Americans; however, he was closely connected with British officialdom. Logan's essay "Of the State of the British Plantations in America," which gives a full statement of his imperialist views, was written only in 1732; see Joseph E. Johnson, "A Quaker Imperialist's View of the British Colonies in America: 1732," *Pennsylvania Magazine of History and Biography*, vol. LX (1936), pp. 97-130.

In these later decades of the first half of the eighteenth century, there was a gradual emergence of a new, more imperialist outlook among the colonists. This development reached its culmination in the Albany Plan of 1754. On the origin of the Albany Plan, see L. H. Gipson, *The British Empire before the American Revolution*, vol. V, New York 1942, chapters 4 and 5. The still disputed issue of the part which Franklin and Massachusetts played in the drafting of the plan is of no particular relevance in our context. The failure of the plan, however, is a sign of how strong colonial resistance against an integrated policy in North America had remained. Alison G. Olson, "The British Government and Colonial Union," *William and Mary Quarterly*, Third Series, vol. XVII (1960), pp. 22-34, shows that, in the middle of the eighteenth century, circles in England also had become doubtful regarding the usefulness of greater collaboration among the colonies because the trend towards independence might be strengthened.

CHAPTER II: INSULA FORTUNATA

This chapter represents a thoroughly revised—in part abbreviated, in part enlarged—version of my article "The English Background of American Isolationism in the Eighteenth Century," *William and Mary Quarterly*, Third Series, vol. i (1944), pp. 138-160.

1. English ideas on foreign policy in the eighteenth century and the emergence of an isolationist outlook in England

The *Bibliography of British History: The Eighteenth Century 1714-1789*, ed. S. Pargellis and D. J. Medley, Oxford 1951, shows the thoroughness with which this period of English history has been studied. In recent years, under the influence of Sir Lewis Namier and his school, the attention of scholars has focussed on the "structure of politics" in this period, and the history of diplomacy, which had aroused the chief interest of scholars of the preceding generation, has been somewhat neglected. Thus, in the field of foreign affairs, the well-known works of older scholars like Sir Richard Lodge are still basic. Of more recent works, those by Richard Pares—*War and Trade in the West Indies, 1739-1763*, London 1936, and "American versus Continental Warfare 1739-63," *English Historical Review*, vol. li (1936), pp. 429-465—are relevant. For Sir Robert Walpole, see the biography by J. H. Plumb. However, the contemporary interpretation of the intentions of men like Walpole and Carteret rather than their actual intentions are of interest for this book.

For the description of the public debate on foreign policy I have used Cobbett's *Parliamentary History of England* and pamphlets. The question whether Cobbett's reports about the speeches in the House of Common and the House of Lords are precise in every detail is of no relevance in our context. My study of the pamphlet literature, although certainly not exhaustive, was comprehensive enough, I hope, to permit the outline of main trends as given in the text [pp. 24-32]. A systematic scholarly analysis of political pamphleteering in eighteenth century England is not available. William E. H. Lecky, in his *History of England in the Eighteenth Century*, makes extensive use of pamphlets. W. T. Laprade, *Public Opinion and Politics in Eighteenth Century England*, New York 1936, reproduces the content of a great number of newspapers and pamphlets from the first quarter of the eighteenth century. A. M. Wilson, *French Foreign Policy . . . of Cardinal Fleury, 1726-43*, Cambridge 1936, discusses a few single pamphlets of particular significance. Richard Pares, in the abovementioned article "American versus Continental Warfare 1739-63," enters into a thorough discussion of the pamphlet literature concerned with this problem. On the importance of Mauduit's *Considerations on the present German War*, see also Basil Williams, *Life of William Pitt, Earl of Chatham*, London 1914, and Brian Turnstall, *William Pitt, Earl of Chatham*, London 1938.

I have refrained from suggesting names of authors for these anonymous pamphlets; without a systematic investigation of this literature, we cannot be sure whether the ascriptions of authorship which one finds in the eighteenth century are correct. However, Chesterfield's authorship (together with Waller) of *The case of the Hanover Forces* [p. 26] is certain.

2. *The reception of these ideas in America: Paine's "Common Sense"*

Interesting material on Americans in England shortly before the War of Independence [pp. 33-34] will be found in Benjamin Rush, *Letters*, ed. L. H. Butterfield, vol. I, Princeton 1951; these letters show clearly the eminent role of Franklin among Americans in England. For Franklin's part in the discussion on peace terms during the Seven Years' War [p. 34], see Gerald Stourzh, *Benjamin Franklin and American Foreign Policy*, pp. 65-82 and the literature quoted there. On James Burgh [p. 35], who, despite his fame and influence in the eighteenth century, has been almost completely neglected in the scholarly literature, see now Caroline Robbins, *The Eighteenth-Century Commonwealthman*, Cambridge 1959, particularly pp. 364-368; the book should be generally consulted for the influence of English radical thought on American political thinking.

On Paine, see the article by Crane Brinton in *Dictionary of American Biography*. For the situation in Philadelphia, when *Common Sense* was written [pp. 38-40], see A. M. Schlesinger, *The Colonial Merchants and the American Revolution*, New York 1939, Merrill Jensen, *The Articles of Confederation*, Madison 1940, and John C. Miller, *The Origins of the American Revolution*, Boston 1943, who, on p. 467, states that before *Common Sense*, the revolutionary movement "was slowly congealing" [p. 40]. On the significance of the Bible story of Saul and Samuel for European republicanism [p. 41], see P. Kirn, "Saul in der Staatslehre," *Festschrift fuer Erich Brandenburg*, Leipzig 1928, pp. 28-47. For the importance of the distinction between a "complex" and a "simple" structure of government [p. 41], see Elie Halévy, *La Formation du Radicalism Philosophique*, vol. II, Paris 1901, pp. 54-56, and also Priestley, *An Essay on the First Principles of Government and on the Nature of political, civil and religious liberty*, London 1771, p. 19. For the close relation between Priestley and Paine [pp. 41-42], Priestley, *op.cit.*, pp. 6-8 should be compared with Thomas Paine, *Complete Writings*, ed. Philip S. Foner, vol. I, New York 1945, pp. 5-6; see also Priestley, *op.cit.*, pp. 12, 18-19, 40, 42. For an interesting condemnation of traditional diplomacy by Priestley, see his *Letters to the Inhabitants of*

Northumberland, published in 1799, especially Letter xii and the appended Maxims.

CHAPTER III: NOVUS ORDO SECULORUM

Sections of this chapter, though thoroughly revised, correspond to sections of my article, "The New Diplomacy of the Eighteenth Century," *World Politics*, vol. iv (1951), pp. 1-38.

1. The question of "foreign alliances" in 1776 and the Model Treaty

The beginnings of American diplomacy, as far as the factual developments are concerned, are described in all histories of the early years of the United States; a detailed authoritative treatment is that by S. F. Bemis, *The Diplomacy of the American Revolution*, New York 1935. However, my special concern in this section—the analysis of the conceptual framework which determined the first American actions in foreign policy—has not been scrutinized in an equally thorough manner.

John Adams played a decisive role in these early developments. He is usually regarded as a rigid isolationist from the beginning of his political career to the end of his life. There can be no doubt that, in later years, Adams tried to represent himself as the "father" of American isolationism. However, if one limits the analysis of Adams's early ideas exclusively to contemporary material and refrains from using Adams's later, somewhat tendentious utterances, a somewhat different picture emerges. Adams appears to have shared the hopes and fears of the majority of the Congress regarding the entry of the United States into the field of foreign affairs; isolationism and internationalism were then not conceived as excluding each other. Some scholars have made suggestions along the line of interpretation which I have given, see Gilbert Chinard, *Honest John Adams*, Boston 1933, p. 88; also

Wharton in his introduction to *The Revolutionary Diplomatic Correspondence of the United States*, vol. i, Washington 1889, pp. 511-513. Gerald Stourzh, *Benjamin Franklin and American Foreign Policy*, Chicago 1954, p. 287, note 39, suggests that Adams did not change his views but used only a "sharper terminology" in later years. I am unable to accept this point of view; as, for instance, Adams's attitude to the problem of etiquette [p. 77], shows, he underwent a change in his entire political approach. On the various "phases" through which Adams passed, see also Joseph Charles, "The Origins of the American Party System," *William and Mary Quarterly*, Third Series, vol. xii (1955), pp. 421-422.

The following remarks refer to details discussed in this section:

The interesting but somewhat unexplained note which Adams wrote in March 1776 [p. 49] was composed at the time when Silas Deane was leaving for France; it may have been a reminder of oral instructions given to Deane before his departure.

The statement that Franklin put into Adams's hands "a printed volume of treaties" [p. 50] comes from Adams's Diary. Although this part of Adams's Diary is not contemporary with the events which it reports, there seems little reason to doubt the authenticity of such a detail.

My article, "The 'New Diplomacy' of the Eighteenth Century," *loc.cit.*, p. 25, note 74, provides a detailed comparison of the clauses of the Model Treaty with the clauses of the treaties of 1686 and 1713 between England and France. For proof of my statement that Adams relied heavily on these two treaties in drafting the Model Treaty [p. 50], the reader is referred to this article.

2. The ideas of the French philosophes on foreign policy and on a "new diplomacy"

Franco Venturi, "L'Illuminismo nel Settecento Europeo,"

XI Congrès International des Sciences Historiques, Rapports, vol. IV (Histoire Moderne), Uppsala 1960, pp. 106-135, provides the most recent general survey of enlightenment thought; the author stresses the connection between the ideas of the philosophes and the French social situation [p. 58].

The rich literature on the enlightenment has somewhat neglected the views of the philosophes on foreign policy and diplomacy. For instance, the standard work on the Physiocrats—Georges Weulersse, *Le Mouvement Physiocratique en France*, Paris 1910—touches upon this subject only quite briefly and generally in vol. II, pp. 100-106. The neglect of this aspect of enlightenment thinking is entirely comprehensible because the philosophes themselves regarded the issues of foreign policy as of secondary importance in comparison to those of domestic policy.

However, some facts of the problem with which this section deals are treated in the literature which is concerned with the importance of the eighteenth century for the development of the idea of eternal peace. For the ideas of peace in the Encyclopédie, see Eberhard Weiss, *Geschichtsschreibung und Staatsauffassung in der Franzoesischen Enzyclopaedie*, Wiesbaden 1958. Among the more general books on the idea of eternal peace, I mention here Carl Joachim Friedrich, *Inevitable Peace*, Cambridge 1948, Kurt von Raumer, *Ewiger Friede*, Freiburg 1953 and Elizabeth V. Souleyman, *The Vision of World Peace in Seventeenth and Eighteenth Century France*, New York 1941. However, the figures which are most prominently treated in these works—the Abbé St. Pierre, Rousseau, Kant—are of less importance in our context because these thinkers had little interest in the technical aspects of the functioning of diplomacy and in its reform.

I have tried to focus on the common features in the thinking of the philosophes on diplomacy and foreign affairs. Although among them, particularly among the Physiocrats, the conformity of thinking is very great, some of the philosophes have a very individual approach. For instance Mably, although extremely critical of the conduct of diplomacy, had less illusions about the approach of a new peaceful era than the other philosophes. Mably's very original mind cannot easily be fitted into any school of thinking; see Ernest A. Whitfield, *Gabriel Bonnot de Mably*, London 1930. In my article "The 'New Diplomacy' of the Eighteenth Century," I have made a greater attempt to analyze the extent to which differences in their general approach modified the views of the philosophes regarding foreign affairs than in this chapter where it seemed enough to emphasize the basic common features.

3. The influence of idealist and internationalist ideas on the conduct of early American foreign policy

The fundamental assumption of this chapter—common outlook of European and American thinkers in the second part of the eighteenth century—has been stressed by Michael Kraus, *The Atlantic Civilization, Eighteenth Century Origins*, Ithaca 1949, and has been recently illuminated in a much broader context by Robert R. Palmer, *The Age of the Democratic Revolution. A Political History of Europe and America*, Princeton 1959; there is on pp. 269-270 an analysis of Mably's attitude toward America and of his contacts with John Adams [p. 66]. Emphasis on the intellectual unity of the Atlantic community does not invalidate the point which Louis Hartz, *The Liberal Tradition in America*, New York 1955, makes that the same ideas might take a different development in America because they were planted in a very different setting as, in contrast to Europe, America had no feudal past. This remark is more relevant, however, for the development of social and constitutional ideas than for those on diplomacy, but see section v of the last chapter of this book.

In addition to works previously listed, and to works which will be named below in the bibliographical essay to Chapter v, I would like here to state my obligation to Dumas Malone, *Jefferson and his Time*, Boston 1948. I found suggestive remarks also in Adrienne Koch, *Jefferson and Madison; the Great Collaboration*, New York 1950, and I used with profit the older book by Otto Vossler, *Die amerikanischen Revolutionsideale in ihrem Verhaeltnis zu den europaeischen, untersucht an Thomas Jefferson*, Muenchen 1929, to which Robert R. Palmer directed attention in his article "A Neglected Work: Otto Vossler on Jefferson and the Revolutionary Era," *William and Mary Quarterly*, Third Series, vol. xii (1955), pp. 462-471. Description of the role which Jefferson played in drafting the report for Congress in 1784 and in the negotiations with Prussia [pp. 70-72] was facilitated by the copious editorial notes to be found in *The Papers of Thomas Jefferson*, ed. Julian P. Boyd. Since this edition has not advanced beyond the year 1789, older editions of Jefferson's works had to be used for documentation of views Jefferson expressed in later years.

CHAPTER IV: RATIO STATUS

1. The development of a diplomatic bureaucracy in America

The salient facts about the introduction of ceremonial forms in American political life can be found in most histories of the period. For instance, the story about John Adams's characterization of Washington's address as "His Most Gracious speech" [p. 78] in Morison and Comager, *The Growth of the American Republic*, New York 1942, p. 329. An important contemporary testimony for the indignation of the Radicals about this weakening of the genuine republican spirit is William MacLay, *Journal*, ed. E. S. Maclay, New York 1927. The process of introducing a more formal etiquette in diplomacy can be observed through a study of *The Revolutionary Diplomatic Correspondence of the United States*, ed. Francis Wharton, and the introduction of this work, written by Wharton, remains of great value for assembling the chief data on the establishment of a bureaucratic procedure in the conduct of American foreign affairs. The standard work on this subject is Gaillard Hunt, *The Department of State of the United States; its history and function*, New Haven 1914; but see also Leonard D. White, *The Federalists*, New York 1948, chapter II; Samuel Flagg Bemis, *The Diplomacy of the American Revolution*, New York 1935, and the collection *The American Secretaries of State and their diplomacy*, ed. S. F. Bemis, New York 1927-29, particularly vol. I which contains essays on Livingston and John Jay. I am obligated to the essay on Livingston for the description of his role in the organization of *American diplomacy* [pp. 82-83]; this volume, p. 120, was also used for describing the external working conditions in the Department of State during this period [p. 83]. The connection between the establishment of executive departments and the struggle in the Congress between Radicals and Moderates [pp. 81-82] has been elucidated by Merrill Jensen, *The New Nation; a history of the United States during the Confederation, 1781-1789*, New York 1950.

2. Diplomacy as a science in Europe; the literature of the "interests of the states" and of the "Political Testaments"

As the great language dictionaries indicate, the word "diplomacy" in its modern technical sense [p. 92] was first used in the eighteenth century. The derivation from Leibniz' *Codex juris gentium diplomaticus* seems likely [p. 94], although other derivations have been suggested. A stimulating guide to the general problems of diplomacy, with a brief bibliography, is Harold Nicolson, *Diplomacy*, London, New York 1939. Some interesting remarks on diplomacy, which have their bearing on the eighteenth century, will be found in G. N. Clark, *The Seventeenth Century*, Oxford 1931, sections 8 and 10; on p. 134, Clark mentions the various training schools for diplomats which were founded in the eighteenth century [pp. 93-94]. About the academy, directed by Koch and Schoepflin in Strassburg, and its various students [p. 94], see H. von Srbik, *Metternich: Der Staatsmann und der Mensch*, Muenchen 1957, vol. I, p. 65, and, for bibliography on this academy, vol. III, p. 41. In addition to the famous collections of treaties mentioned in the text [p. 95], there were numerous others; one was edited by Koch and Schoepflin. Mably's *Droit Public* served the same purpose of providing a guide through the existing alliance and treaty systems. Of course, some important collections of documents were undertaken in previous centuries, but the development was brought to a high point in the eighteenth century.

The same must be said regarding the doctrine of the interests of the states. Prince Henri de Rohan, a figure of the seventeenth century, is usually regarded as its originator. He was then followed by Courtilz de Sandras, who, in turn, was followed by Rousset de Missy. This genealogy of the school is provided by Rousset himself in the preface to his book *Les Intérêts Présens des Puissances de l'Europe*, Hague 1733. He does not mention the interesting essay by Vauban, *Intérêt Présent des Etats de la Chrétienté*, written in the typical spirit of the school. Rohan, Courtilz de Sandras, and Rousset are the three writers to whom special chapters are devoted in Friedrich Meinecke, *Die Idee der Staatsraeson in der Neueren Geschichte*, Muenchen-Berlin 1924 (translated into English under the title *Machiavellism*, New York 1957). This book gives the only comprehensive treatment of the doctrine of the interests of the states, and my presentation is indebted to Meinecke's analysis. Meinecke was interested in the doctrine of the interests of the states from the point of view of its significance for the relation between morals and politics; my point of emphasis is the attempt of these writers to make power politics rational. It is impossible to claim that the writings of this school are particularly original or interesting, but they are representative of a widely spread, typically eighteenth-century viewpoint.

Meinecke was aware of the influence of this school of thinking on Frederick the Great, to whom one of the most important chapters of Meinecke's book is devoted. Otherwise, as far as I know, the relation between the doctrine of the interests of the states and the vogue for Political Testaments in the eighteenth century has never been pointed out. Again, it should be stated that Political Testaments are not new in the seventeenth and eighteenth centuries; they can be traced back to earlier times and may have had classical ancestors in the mirror-of-princes literature. Nevertheless, in their pure form—as documents which were not concerned with distribution of property and possessions but exclusively devoted to political issues and to the explanation of principles which ought to guide politics—Political Testaments were a product of the period which we are considering. The first Political Testament in this sense was probably that of Richelieu. The form which Richelieu wanted to give to his Political Testament has not yet been satisfactorily established; see Josef Engel, "Zur Frage der Echtheit von Richelieu's 'Testament Politique,'" *Aus Mittelalter und Neuzeit: Festschrift G. Kallen*, Bonn 1957. Richelieu's Political Testament was published in the seventeenth century in a distorted form; in general, however, authentic Political Testaments by rulers and statesmen—like those of Frederick the Great—remained secret. Published Political Testaments were usually falsifications; there appeared on the book market Political Testaments by Alberoni, Colbert, Walpole, Louvois, Mazarin, the Duke of Lorrain, Jan de Witt, Peter the Great, and others. Some of them are pure propaganda, like the *Testament Politique du Chevalier Walpole*, Amsterdam 1767, which is an anti-Hanoverian tract. Some, like that of Louvois, are historical accounts of the events in which their "authors" had played a role, but others like that of Jan de Witt make a serious attempt to analyze the policy of a country in terms of the doctrine of the interests of the state. Collections containing several Political Testaments were popular in the eighteenth century; see, for instance, the *Recueil des Testamens Politiques*, 4 vols., Amsterdam 1749, which was edited by Courtilz de Sandras—a confirmation of the close connection between the doctrine of the interests of the states and the Political Testaments.

Concerning the influence of the doctrine of the interests of the states on modern diplomatic history [p. 104], there is an obvious relation to Ranke, to his concept of the Great Powers and of the primacy of foreign policy.

3. The role of America in European diplomatic thinking: Thomas Pownall

This section is based on two articles by Max Savelle, "Colonial Origins of American Diplomatic Principles," *Pacific Historical Review*, vol. III (1934), pp. 334-350, and "The American Balance of Power and European Diplomacy 1713-1778" in *The Era of the American Revolution. Studies inscribed to E. B. Greene*, New York 1939, pp. 140-169, on the book by A. Rein, *Der Kampf Westeuropas um Nordamerika im 15. und 16. Jahrhundert*, Stuttgart 1925, and on Rein's article "Ueber die Bedeutung der ueberseeischen Ausdehnung fuer das europaeische Staatensystem," *Historische Zeitschrift*, vol. CXXXVII (1928), pp. 28-90. See also Edward S. Corwin, *French Policy and the American Alliance*, Princeton 1916, which discusses the influence of the idea of balance of power on the French attitude in the time of the American Revolution.

Thomas Pownall's career in America has been treated by J. A. Schutz, *Thomas Pownall, British Defender of American Liberty*, Glendale 1951. A characterization of Pownall's political views will be found in Caroline Robbins, *The Eighteenth-Century Commonwealthman*, Cambridge 1959, particularly pp. 311-318; on p. 435 a bibliographical note on Pownall. The "Memorial to the Sovereigns of Europe" has found little attention in the scholarly literature; for Adams's use of this pamphlet [p. 110], see his letter printed in John Adams, *Works*, vol. VII, Boston 1852, p. 348.

4. Alexander Hamilton as representative of European political realism

References to older literature have been made superfluous through the two recent Hamilton biographies: Broadus Mitchell, *Alexander Hamilton: Youth to Maturity 1755-1788*, New York 1957, and John C. Miller, *Alexander Hamilton: Portrait in Paradox*, New York 1959; these two books are political biographies rather than studies in intellectual history. Indications of the intellectual influences which formed Hamilton's mind are given in Alexander Bein, *Die Staatsidee von Alexander Hamilton*, Muenchen Berlin 1927. Hamilton's list of reading [p. 111] is printed in Alexander Hamilton, *Works*, ed. John C. Hamilton, vol. I, New York 1851, p. 4.

CHAPTER V: THE FAREWELL ADDRESS

The factual background of this chapter is well established in a large number of books and studies. The manuscript of this book was completed before John C. Miller, *The Federalist Era 1789-1901, New American Nation Series*, New York 1960, was published but I might refer the reader to its critical bibliography. Recent studies like Alexander De-

Conde, *Entangling Alliance*, Durham 1958, or the articles
by Joseph Charles, "The Origins of the American Party
System," *William and Mary Quarterly*, Third Series, vol. xii
(1955), emphasize the connection between diplomatic
events and the domestic political struggle and make the
Farewell Address an expression of Hamiltonian Federalism.
Although I agree in general with this stress on Hamilton's
role, it should not be overlooked that Washington had a
mind of his own and saw things in a broader frame of reference. Hamilton had to take this into account.

Fundamental for a study of the origin of the Farewell
Address is the book by Victor Hugo Paltsits, *Washington's
Farewell Address*, New York 1935. Paltsits publishes the
various documents which have bearing on the composition
of the Farewell Address and gives the full text of its different versions. The texts which I publish in the Appendix
[pp. 137-147] are taken from Paltsits' book and I am grateful
to its publisher, the New York Public Library, for permission to reproduce these texts. Like all students of the subject, I am deeply obligated to Paltsits' work; without it my
analysis of the Farewell Address would have been impossible.

Nevertheless the very thoroughness of Paltsits' work has
had its disadvantages. Because of the "authoritative" character of Paltsits' story and interpretation, further investigation has been regarded as superfluous. Paltsits' results have
simply been embodied in descriptions of these years. A
curious, extreme case is Nathan Schachner, *Alexander Hamilton*, New York 1946, p. 354, who refers to Paltsits' account
as "definitive," but presents a story which is very different
and widely erroneous.

Recognition of the great merits of Paltsits' book should
not stultify further research; neither its factual part nor its
interpretative part ought to be regarded as "final."

BIBLIOGRAPHICAL ESSAY

I deviate from Paltsits and previous discussions of the origin of the Farewell Address in one point of fact. Paltsits, p. 31, puts the conversation, in which Washington broached to Hamilton the subject of a valedictory address "shortly before May 10, 1796." I place this conversation in February [p. 119]. We know that Hamilton was in February in Philadelphia to appear as witness before Court and that he attended the celebrations of Washington's birthday; see John C. Hamilton, *Life of Alexander Hamilton. A History of the Republic of the United States of America*, vol. vi, Boston 1879, pp. 343-344. There is no proof that Hamilton travelled again to Philadelphia in the spring of the same year. Hamilton's letters indicate that, during March, April, and the first days of May, he cannot have been away from New York for any length of time. There is a short gap in his correspondence from May 5 to May 9, but on May 4 Hamilton addressed a letter to Rufus King in Philadelphia, and this makes it unlikely that he intended to travel to Philadelphia within the next day. Washington wrote a letter to Hamilton on May 8, see Paltsits, pp. 241-243, and he would not have done this if he had just met, or was expecting to meet, Hamilton in Philadelphia. Thus not only direct proof for a trip by Hamilton to Philadelphia after February is lacking; it seems almost impossible to fit such a trip into Hamilton's schedule. The reason why it had been suggested that Hamilton went to Philadelphia "shortly before May 10" is that Hamilton begins his letter to Washington of May 10 with saying: "When last in Philadelphia . . . ," but I cannot see that this remark necessitates the assumption of a trip at the beginning of May. This sentence makes quite as much, if not better, sense, if taken as referring to his meeting with Washington in February. Moreover, another sentence in this letter, beginning "A few days since . . . ," is hardly compatible with a recent meeting

[167]

between Washington and Hamilton. In February, there had been a lot of talk about Washington's retirement, as Madison's letter to Monroe of February 26, 1796 indicates. It might be added that, also in 1792, Washington had given some thought to his retirement around the time of his birthday.

Washington's letter to Gouverneur Morris [p. 122], which is very close to Washington's draft, ought to be added to the material which Paltsits, p. 39, mentions as foreshadowing the ideas which Washington put into his draft.

On Washington's dinner with Madison in May 1796 [p. 125], see J. A. Carroll and H. W. Ashworth (continuing the biography of Douglas Southall Freeman), *George Washington*, vol. vii, New York 1957, p. 381, but it must be stated that, although we have Washington's invitation to Madison, concrete proof that the dinner took place is lacking.

I differ from Paltsits mainly in questions of interpretation. Paltsits' account is a vindication of Washington as the true author of the Farewell Address. Paltsits suggests that Madison and Hamilton were only carrying out carefully and precisely Washington's instructions. Paltsits concentrates on the correspondence between Washington and Hamilton, which shows Washington in a directing role, rather than on a comparison of the various versions from which the final form of the Farewell Address developed. I have tried to show that Hamilton's contribution went beyond an execution of Washington's instructions and added a new intellectual element.

This does not mean that I want to claim Hamilton as author of the Farewell Address. It seems sound procedure to regard as author of a document a man who signed it and took responsibility for it. Moreover, the general ideas, and in the first half of the Farewell Address, even the wording remained close to Washington's and Madison's draft. Finally, Washington went over Hamilton's Major Draft most care-fully and made many stylistic changes. "Washington in col-laboration with Madison and Hamilton" might be the most correct formulation of the authorship of this document. We know little about the part which Jay played who had been consulted by Hamilton.

Literature on the impact of the Farewell Address is listed in the *Harvard Guide to American History*, Cambridge 1954; through the adumbration of the idea of the separation of spheres, the Farewell Address forms part of the history of the genesis of the Monroe Doctrine.

Index

INDEX